P9-BZH-232

Social Issues
in Literature

Race in Mark Twain's
Adventures of
Huckleberry Finn

Other Books in the Social Issues in Literature Series:

Social Issues
in Literature

Race in Mark Twain's *Adventures of Huckleberry Finn*

Claudia Durst Johnson, Book Editor

GREENHAVEN PRESS

A part of Gale, Cengage Learning

GALE
CENGAGE Learning·

Detroit • New York • San Francisco • New Haven, Conn • Waterville, Maine • London

GALE
CENGAGE Learning™

Christine Nasso, *Publisher*
Elizabeth Des Chenes, *Managing Editor*

© 2009 Greenhaven Press, a part of Gale, Cengage Learning

Gale and Greenhaven Press are registered trademarks used herein under license.

For more information, contact:
Greenhaven Press
27500 Drake Rd.
Farmington Hills, MI 48331-3535
Or you can visit our Internet site at gale.cengage.com

For product information and technology assistance, contact us at

Gale Customer Support, 1-800-877-4253
For permission to use material from this text or product, submit all requests online at www.cengage.com/permissions

Further permissions questions can be emailed to permissionrequest@cengage.com

Articles in Greenhaven Press anthologies are often edited for length to meet page requirements. In addition, original titles of these works are changed to clearly present the main thesis and to explicitly indicate the author's opinion. Every effort is made to ensure that Greenhaven Press accurately reflects the original intent of the authors. Every effort has been made to trace the owners of copyrighted material.

Cover image © John Springer Collection/Corbis.

LIBRARY OF CONGRESS CATALOGING-IN-PUBLICATION DATA

Race in Mark Twain's Adventures of Huckleberry Finn / Claudia Durst Johnson, book editor.
      p. cm. -- (Social issues in literature)
   Includes bibliographical references and index.
   ISBN 978-0-7377-4616-7 (hardcover)
   ISBN 978-0-7377-4617-4 (pbk.)
   1. Twain, Mark, 1835-1910. Adventures of Huckleberry Finn--Juvenile literature.
   2. Twain, Mark, 1835-1910--Juvenile literature. 3. Race relations in literature--Juvenile literature. I. Johnson, Claudia Durst.
   PS1305.R33 2009
   813'.4--dc22
                                                        2009014563

Printed in the United States of America
1 2 3 4 5 6 7 13 12 11 10 09

Contents

Chapter 1: The Life of Mark Twain

Chapter 2: Race in *Huck Finn*

Chapter 3: Issues of Race in the Twenty-First Century

Introduction

In exploring the issue of race in Mark Twain's *Adventures of Huckleberry Finn* and its implications in the twenty-first century, one is obliged to come to terms with what Abraham Lincoln saw as the curse of the country. Slavery was a part of the New World society from the beginning, at first with minimal regard to race. Poor Englishmen were brought to the colonies as virtual slaves—indentured servants who belonged to their masters until they could buy their freedom. For the time of their contracted labor, young apprentices lived in slavery as they learned a trade. Many nineteenth-century reformers called white factory workers and tenant farmers little better than slaves whose pay was too low to live on, who worked for fourteen hours or more every day of the week, and whose debts tied them to their employers.

But the legal slavery that began in colonial America with the importation of slaves from Africa in 1619 and lasted until the Emancipation Proclamation in 1863, was based on race, and the distinctions between the laws governing black slaves and white workers were significant. With the exception of a small population of "freedmen," African Americans in the United States were enslaved by law. They were bought and sold, often at auction, like cattle. Their families were separated in the process of buying and selling. According to the "Black Code" of 1664, they were slaves for life. Not only were African Americans defined as property for life by law, but their children, grandchildren, and great grandchildren were also slaves for life.

Some would argue that, as property, black slaves were sometimes better cared for by their masters than white workers were. But African American slaves were not legally free. As Twain's character Jim points out, slaves did not own themselves. They were routinely beaten, tortured, and maimed for minor infractions. They were bred to other slaves like cattle and were forbidden to marry, to learn to read and write, and to form religious groups. It was against the law in slave territory for a white person to teach a black slave to read. The sexual assaults that plagued white working-class women were magnified on a massive scale on plantations where owners raped their black slaves and sold the offspring for profit. Some slaves were well cared for, but no slave owned him- or herself.

It was generally understood that the farther south one went, the worse conditions were for African American slaves. Being sold "down river" (the Mississippi), to New Orleans, to be auctioned off was usually a slave's worst nightmare.

This is the setting of Mark Twain's *Adventures of Huckleberry Finn*—the nineteenth-century slave-holding culture in the United States. Sam Clemens, who later assumed the pen name of Mark Twain, lived in slave territory on the Mississippi River and as a riverboat captain until he was twenty-six years old; he observed the fate of runaway slaves while he worked on what was a central route of slave trafficking.

The issue of race in *Adventures of Huckleberry Finn* has been controversial from the time of its publication in 1884 to the present day, having been banned in Concord, Massachusetts, just after it was published and remaining to this day one of the most frequently challenged books. The fundamental argument about race in the novel is whether or not it is a racist work or an antiracist work. For years the issue of race in *Adventures of Huckleberry Finn* was ignored. It was considered a boy's book, a simple, amusing adventure story, without interest for the adult reader, much less literary specialists. Not until many years after its publication did literary critics begin reading the novel, discovering that not only is race the central issue, but far from being a carefree boy's book, it is one of our darkest visions of human nature and society.

What complicates the interpretation of *Adventures of Huckleberry Finn* is that the story is told by an ironic narrator. The voice of the author and that of the narrator are not identical, and we, as readers, end up knowing more about the characters and Huck's experience than Huck does. Huck is generally seen as an innocent who, while he never intellectually condemns racism and the slaveholding society in which he has been raised, acts from his heart to defy the church and the law and thereby, he thinks, damns himself, in order to save his black friend.

The prevailing interpretation of the novel in the twenty-first century is that Mark Twain, the author, wrote a book that was an attack on slaveholding and racist society. But some readers conclude that Twain's frequent use of the "N-word," Jim's sometimes burlesque character, and the final Tom Sawyer chapters betray it as a racist novel. These arguments are presented and refuted in the essays in this book.

The greatest controversy regarding race centers on the last eleven chapters of the novel, often referred to as the "evasion" sequence, when Tom Sawyer reenters the scene. Huck has decided to defy a society that treated him little better than a slave, with the goal of freeing Jim. But Tom Sawyer, steeped in Southern romanticism, overwhelms Huck's better judgment and makes the escape a torturous, prolonged adventure to lead Huck in freeing Jim, which he hopes will last forever, even though Tom knows Jim has already been freed by his owner.

In the essays that follow, critics argue a variety of points of view about race in the novel. The concluding chapter's essays are on the issue of race in twenty-first-century American society, demonstrating that the issues raised by Twain more than a century ago continue to resonate today.

Chronology

1835

Samuel Langhorne Clemens, the sixth of seven children, is born to Jane Lampton and John Marshall Clemens in Florida, Missouri.

1839

The Clemens family moves to Hannibal, Missouri.

1847

Clemens's father dies.

1848

Clemens begins working as apprentice printer.

1857–1861

Clemens is a riverboat pilot on the Mississippi.

1861

The Civil War begins; Clemens serves briefly in a Confederate army unit, then (in July) accompanies brother Orion to Nevada.

1862–1864

Clemens works as a reporter for the *Territorial Enterprise,* Virginia City, Nevada.

1863

Clemens first uses the pen name Mark Twain.

1864–1867

Clemens works as a reporter for the *San Francisco Morning Call.*

1865

Instant success comes with the publication of the story "Jim Smiley and His Jumping Frog."

1867

Clemens moves to New York City.

1869

The Innocents Abroad is published.

1870

Clemens marries Olivia Langdon, daughter of a wealthy coal merchant.

1871

The Clemens family moves to Nook Farm, Connecticut.

1872

Clemens's two-year-old son, Langdon, dies.

1873

Clemens and Charles Dudley Warner's jointly written novel *The Gilded Age* is published.

1874

"A True Story" is published, earning Clemens recognition as a serious writer.

1876

The Adventures of Tom Sawyer is published; Clemens begins a sequel (about Tom's friend Huck Finn), but stalls around chapter 16 and waits for new inspiration.

1880

A Tramp Abroad is published.

1881

The Prince and the Pauper is published.

1883

Life on the Mississippi is published.

1884

Adventures of Huckleberry Finn is published.

1889

A Connecticut Yankee in King Arthur's Court is published.

1894

Pudd'nhead Wilson is published.

1896

Personal Recollections of Joan of Arc is published.
Clemens's daughter Susy dies.

1904

After years of illness, Clemens's wife, Olivia, dies in Florence, Italy.

1906

What Is Man? is published anonymously in an edition of just 250 copies.

1909

Clemens's daughter Jean dies.

1910

Clemens dies on April 21, at Redding, Connecticut.

1916

The Mysterious Stranger is published posthumously.

Social Issues in Literature

CHAPTER 1

The Life of Mark Twain

A River Child, a Wanderer, an Outcast

Pascal Covici Jr.

Pascal Covici Jr. was E.A. Lilly Professor in American Literature at Southern Methodist University and the author of Humor and Revelation in American Literature. *He died in February 2009.*

Samuel Clemens grew up in the slaveholding upper South. His boyhood was spent in Hannibal, Missouri, on the Mississippi River, in a setting not unlike that of his most famous character, Huck Finn. A roamer like Huck Finn, he worked as a Mississippi riverboat pilot and a reporter out west. He eventually settled down with his wife in Hartford, Connecticut. His neighbor there was Harriet Beecher Stowe, author of Uncle Tom's Cabin. *Clemens, who wrote under the name of Mark Twain, always felt he was an imposter in the Northeast. In Hartford he eventually found his voice as a writer, publishing "A True Story," told by an ex-slave whose family had been sold. His bitterness against society, behind the comedy of* The Adventures of Huckleberry Finn, *grew increasingly intense with the works that followed.*

Mark Twain's work captures the child that lives in the American psyche and also presents the confusions of the American adult. As a mature writer, Twain could recreate the small-town boyhood he had known by the Mississippi River in those halcyon [peaceful] years before the Civil War. His philosophical ponderings, however, kept leading him back to simple views of mankind as either deservedly damned or irresponsibly determined, and then, finally as a figment of some celestial imagination, "wandering forlorn among the

Pascal Covici Jr., "Mark Twain (Samuel Langhorne Clemens)," in *Dictionary of Literary Biography, vol. 11, American Humorists, 1800–1950,* Detroit, MI: Gale, 1982, pp. 526–555. Copyright © 1982 Gale Research Company. Reproduced by permission of Gale, a part of Cengage Learning.

empty eternities," disillusioned with the world in which he finds himself but unable to make his way to any other. Mark Twain is best known for his evocations of pre–Civil War life along the Mississippi in *The Adventures of Tom Sawyer* (1876), *Life on the Mississippi* (1883), and *The Adventures of Huckleberry Finn* (1884). Still, readers have cherished almost as much his books of wandering, whether factually based travel books, such as *The Innocents Abroad* (1869), *Roughing It* (1872), *A Tramp Abroad* (1880), and *Following the Equator* (1897) or fiction like *A Connecticut Yankee in King Arthur's Court* (1889), and his later bitter contemplations of the human heart: *Pudd'nhead Wilson* (1894), "The Man That Corrupted Hadleyburg" (1900), and *The Mysterious Stranger* (1916), unfinished at the time of his death. Clemens/Twain became, to an extent, that stranger, sickened not only by what he saw as the money-mad society around him but also by his own participation in it. At the same time, he remained, however self-contradictingly, the sensation-loving boy whom he depicted as Tom Sawyer, eager to cause a stir and ready to apologize afterwards. Get-rich-quick schemes, intense personal hatreds arising from business as well as from personal dealings, equally intense loves and loyalties—the emotional nature of the man and his final confusion when the promises of the American Dream of personal satisfaction through financial success turned increasingly into nightmare—have made Mark Twain's life the subject of intensive scholarly research equal in range and in thoroughness to the critical exploration of his written work. We study the life because of the work, but both repay attention.

Samuel Clemens's Childhood

From genteel but shabby beginnings, Samuel Langhorne Clemens rose to both respectability and respect, glad to belong to the wealthy upper reaches of the society that he knew well enough to laugh at while striving, meanwhile, to please. He was born in a town so small that, as he later wrote, he "increased the population by 1 per cent." He liked to jest that he "could have done it for any place—even London, I suppose." His father and mother, John Marshall and Jane Lampton Clemens, had rented a two-room clapboard house in Florida, Missouri, about 100 feet from the store owned by their brother-in-law, John Quarles, whom Twain later immortalized both in *Life on the Mississippi* and in *Mark Twain's Autobiography* (1924). The house still stands in which Sam Clemens was born thirteen days after Halley's Comet reached its perihelion [point nearest the sun]. He often said that just as he came in with the comet, so he would go out with it, and so indeed he did. The comet worked on his imagination, but the house did not. Far more important were both the Quarles farm and the town in which Sam grew up, Hannibal, where the family moved in 1839. Sam, the third of four sons, was the fifth of the six children who kept adding their weight to the slender reed that was the family fortune. (This is not to count the baby boy, Pleasants, who lived for only a month or so sometime between the births of Pamela and of Margaret in 1827 and 1830.) John Marshall Clemens, in ill health and repeated financial difficulties, had moved his family from Kentucky to Tennessee and finally to Missouri. The comfortable and warmly affectionate Quarles family—so markedly in contrast with his own, where Samuel Clemens remembered "no outward and visible demonstration of affection"—and the farm itself—its woods, fields, and story-telling slaves—impressed young Sam during his childhood years when he spent his summers back in Florida. The family's final move to Hannibal, some thirty miles off, began the most famous boyhood idyll in American literature. . . .

Mark Twain grew up in a family different from most of its neighbors and in an America that, for most of its ambitious citizens, turned out to be different from what they had anticipated. A conservative Whig in politics and a freethinker in religion, John Clemens (who became justice of the peace in Hannibal in 1842) took his family into a rapidly growing river community that was also conventionally and staunchly religious. . . .

The Drifter

By the age of twenty-five, Sam Clemens seemed to be settling down to the life of a fully licensed [riverboat] pilot. Finding a possible niche had taken him quite a while; he explained his wandering years as the result of the great expectations of future wealth entertained by all the family because of land in Tennessee, 70,000 acres of it, that John Marshall Clemens had owned at his death. . . . Sure of eventual plenty, Twain had allowed himself to drift. He had been an itinerant printer, traveling to St. Louis, New York City, and Philadelphia in 1853, and then a printer and journalist for [brother] Orion's *Keokuk* (Iowa) *Saturday Post* until fall of 1856. Bitten once more by the wander-bug, he contributed a few comic letters to the *Post* as Thomas Jefferson Snodgrass and then set off for South America and, so he hoped, a fortune in cocoa. Instead, he met Horace Bixby, the man who "taught" him the river and made him into a pilot. Then came the Civil War, putting an end to steamboat traffic on the Mississippi. His "The Private History of a Campaign That Failed" (1885) presents one version of his brief service as a volunteer in Confederate ranks—a version that, in various after-dinner speeches, he repeatedly revised— and *Roughing It* tells of his July 1861 stagecoach journey west with his brother Orion, who had been appointed secretary to the governor of the Nevada Territory. Clemens went along, nominally to assist the secretary, in reality for the ride. Miner, prospector, and then casual contributor to the *Virginia City Territorial Enterprise* under the name "Josh," Clemens began to use the name "Mark Twain" on his work early in 1863. He had been a full-time reporter since September 1862. . . .

Marriage

Twain came upon an announcement of the *Quaker City* excursion. Instead of going around the world (as he had planned in San Francisco to do), he suddenly decided to participate in what we would now recognize as the first cruise-ship vacation in modern times. . . .

Aboard the *Quaker City*, Twain met Charles "Charley" Langdon, eighteen-year-old son of an Elmira, New York, coal merchant. . . . Young Langdon showed him a miniature [picture] of his older sister, Olivia. Twain's marriage to her, occurring less than fourteen months after they finally met, has elicited more commentary than any other marriage in American literary circles. . . .

Life in the East

In 1871 the Clemenses moved to Hartford, Connecticut, and to the Nook Farm community of writers, including Charles Dudley Warner and Harriet Beecher Stowe. . . .

The forty years of Twain's life that followed marriage to Livy have become almost as public a property as the fictionalized versions of Clemens's boyhood presented in *Tom Sawyer, Huckleberry Finn*, numerous shorter works, many of the later manuscripts, and the *Autobiography*. The visible surface of this life was inordinately public, most spectacularly in Twain's old age when the author-as-public-figure favored white suits and dramatic entrances. . . .

Finding His Subject

He and neighbor Charles Dudley Warner collaborated on the first extended work of fiction to carry Twain's name, *The Gilded Age* (1873), a title taken over by historians for the corrupt last third of the nineteenth century in America. . . . But *The Gilded Age* did little toward Twain's development as a writer, except as it involved him more deeply in the Nook Farm community. The next step in that development came in

Mark Twain (Samuel Clemens) spent his childhood in Hannibal, Missouri. The childhood home, which influenced a great deal of his writings, is now a museum in his memory. Three Lions/Getty Images.

part as a reaction to that community and in delighted response to a reaction by a valued member of it, the Reverend Joseph Twichell, a good friend who had performed his marriage service and who frequently accompanied Twain on long tramps. . . .

Story of an Ex-slave

In 1874 . . . he was working on a number of other projects, some literary, some financially speculative, and of the former not all were humorous. "A True Story" and "The Curious Republic of Gondour" both ended up in the *Atlantic Monthly*

(November 1874 and October 1875), the latter anonymously because he feared that no one would take it seriously if Mark Twain were known to be the author. "A True Story" presents with earned emotion the suffering and joy of an old slave woman as she tells of her separation from her favorite child at a slave auction and of their reunion twenty-two years later during the Civil War. The brutalities of slavery, understated and presented concretely through the ex-slave's memory, and the use of first-person dialect make the story especially interesting as a precursor of *Huckleberry Finn*. Here, too, are the effects of that emphasis on class and rank, of the false aristocracy that Twain saw as characterizing the antebellum South. (In *Life on the Mississippi* he was to call Sir Walter Scott's medieval romances in large measure responsible for Southern aristocratic pretension and thus for the Civil War itself.). . .

The Theme of Boyhood

One cannot know to what extent Twain's disillusionment with contemporary, corrupt, adult society stimulated his imagination to explore and to recapture the past of his boyhood. He could not, in any case, write effective extended fiction about his present world. His first book-length fictional evocation of the past, *The Adventures of Tom Sawyer*, "simply a hymn, put into prose form to give it a worldly air," has become *the* American boyhood idyll. . . .

Tom Sawyer offers a first glimpse of Huckleberry Finn, the wild huckleberries of Twain's adopted New England joining with the derelict Jimmy Finn, town drunkard of Hannibal in the 1840s, to give a name to Twain's most significant creation.

It appears that as Twain approached the ending to Tom's book late in 1875, he began to feel some awareness of a problem with his, at first, sympathetically portrayed central figure. Tom, although he dares to consort with Huck the outcast, responsibly testifies in court against the murderous Injun Joe and gallantly saves Becky and himself from the cave. Perhaps, then, it should be no surprise that he becomes spokesman for genteel respectability, his escapes from society's trammels having been only temporary, designed as the means of purchasing society's applause. Still, there is a difference between Tom's boyishly conventional flouting of conventions during the body of the story and his final insistence that if Huck is to join Tom Sawyer's gang, he must return to the constricting care of the Widow Douglas, because "Huck, we can't let you into the gang if you ain't respectable, you know." Crestfallen, Huck agrees to "stick to the widder till I rot, Tom; and if I git to be a reg'lar ripper of a robber, and everybody talking 'bout it, I reckon she'll be proud she snaked me in out of the wet." Here the story ends, with Huck's amusing last words taking away some of the sting from Tom's betrayal of what might have seemed to be an espousal of real freedom but that is, instead, just a slight kicking up of the heels before settling into a conventional role. Twain says as much in his two-paragraph conclusion: "Most of the characters that perform in this book still live, and are prosperous and happy. Some day" he may take up their adult lives "and see what sort of men and women they turned out to be." In 1902 he learned that the partial model for Huck Finn, Tom Blankenship, had become a much respected justice of the peace in Montana; but this was merely fact and had nothing to do with Twain's literary imagination. In 1891, when he jotted some notes toward a continuation of Huck's story, one of his thoughts was that "Huck comes back ... crazy" and that "both [Tom and Huck] are desolate, life has been a failure. . . ." By the end of *The Adventures of Huckleberry Finn*, this change of heart seems already signaled. When Tom reveals that Jim is "as free as any cretur that walks this earth," Twain has anticipated through the book's action his own comment in his notebook twenty years later: "The skin of every human being contains a slave."

The Genteel South

The greatest work so far of the American comic imagination, Huck's story begins where Tom's ends, and was begun in the summer of 1876, while Twain was still preparing the latter for publication. "You don't know about me without you have read a book by the name of *The Adventures of Tom Sawyer*," begins Huck, and then adds Twain's indictment of himself: "That book was made by Mr. Mark Twain, and he told the truth, mainly. There was things which he stretched, but mainly he told the truth." As Twain well knew, Huck is being charitable. Huck's own book is itself full of evasions. . . . It is not, however, guilty of the great life that Tom's book revels in, and from which it draws its air of peaceful delight: the lie that evil is external to society, encapsulated in, and therefore easily exorcized by the death of, Injun Joe. In Huck's story evil exists not simply in the institution of slavery or in the exploitations engineered by the King and the Duke, but in the very fabric of genteel civilization that makes possible, in addition to these, the use of people as means to ends, even by that most innocent-seeming representative of the established order, Tom Sawyer himself.

This account makes Twain's result and intention appear to be far more congruent than they probably were. Clearly, the shaping of Huck's story—an involved, complex, uncertain process, documented in Walter Blair's *Mark Twain and HUCK FINN* (1960)—came intuitively rather than by plan. Seven years of irregular effort, punctuated by numerous excursions in other directions, lie behind the finished work. Twain at first wrote pretty steadily. Then, with chapter 16, where a steamboat crushes the raft on which Huck and the runaway slave, Jim, are drifting south, Twain abruptly put aside the manuscript. Why, exactly, Huck's story came so hard to him furnishes material for some of the most interesting biographical, historical, social, and literary speculation in which readers indulge. Twain himself saw the process simply as his own intuitive, or perhaps "hydraulic," way of working, a process that he first discusses in reference to the hiatus in the making of *Tom Sawyer*: "When the manuscript had lain in a pigeon-hole two years I took it out one day and read the last chapter that I had written. It was then that I made the great discovery that when the tank runs dry you've only got to leave it alone and it will fill up again in time while you are asleep—also while you are at work on other things and are quite unaware that this unconscious and profitable cerebration is going on." The revivification of memories of the past, he said especially helped to stimulate the flow. . . .

Humor and Bitterness

The question of why we value what we value was never far from the surface of Twain's fiction. Huck Finn himself finally decides to "go to hell" by committing the major crime of helping a slave escape to freedom. His "sound heart," as Twain characterized it in 1895 notes for a lecture tour, triumphs over his "deformed conscience," but only the author and the reader can see that "the conscience . . . can be trained to approve any wild thing you *want* it to approve if you begin its education early and stick to it." . . .

The extent to which his unconscious evaluation of genteel literary culture spilled over into his consciousness tantalizes readers. That his aggression against that culture was in this case unconscious seems most likely, considering the reversals of feelings he later recorded. That he saw himself, for all his success, as still something of an "imposter" in the East also seems likely. As one of his characters might have put it, contemporary America was "too many" for him. The Missouri boyhood of the conventional Tom Sawyer and then of the subversive Huck Finn, the pre-Elizabethan setting of *The Prince and the Pauper* (1881), the European jaunt served up in *A Tramp Abroad*, and the heavy disillusion that informs the return-to-the-river chapters of *Life on the Mississippi* all point to an increasing unease with his American present. His humor, hilarious in places, was to become increasingly ironic and eventually sardonic. . . .

Twain's writing following *Huckleberry Finn* takes numerous directions. The humor becomes more and more bitter, but its source still lies in the upsetting of clichés and popular complacencies. . . . And in the exposure of the huge and unnoticed gap between what people intend by their actions, what they think they are, and what their actions suggest that they are indeed.

Twain's River Culture

Lewis Leary

The late Lewis Leary was professor of English at the University of North Carolina from 1968 to 1976. He was a prolific author, best known for his book Mark Twain's Wound.

The salient point in Lewis Leary's biographical essay is that Mark Twain portrayed Jim as literally enslaved and Huck as virtually enslaved. The theme is one that influenced writers who saw both adventure and despair in the American experience. The river itself symbolized the good and bad of the frontier, its freedom from convention as well as it dangers: as a boy, Clemens had observed from its banks the flourishing slave trade as families were separated and transported from one place to another. Twain's first stories about the Mississippi, leading up to the writing of Huckleberry Finn, *showed the violence, greed, and injustice of a South that romanticized itself. So while Jim escapes legal slavery at the end, Huck, like Sam Clemens in his youth, struck out for the territory west of the Mississippi—away from the kind of phony civilization that had overtaken the land east of the river.*

Most Americans regard Mark Twain with special affection. They know him as a shaggy man who told stories of boyhood adventures so like their own or those they would like to have had that they become intimately a part of personal experience. His cheerful irreverence and unhurried pace seem antidotes for attitudes to which they necessarily but unwillingly surrender. His is the image of what they like to think Americans have been or can be: humorously perceptive, undeceived by sham, successful in spite of circumstance because of distinctive personal characteristics. . . .

Lewis Leary, "Mark Twain," in *American Writers: A Collection of Literary Biographies*, ed. Leonard Unger, New York: Charles Scribner's Sons, 1974, pp. 190–213. Copyright © 1960–1965, 1968–1971, 1974 by the University of Minnesota. Reproduced by permission of Gale, a part of Cengage Learning.

Twain's Influence

No wonder then that Ernest Hemingway found all American literature to begin with Mark Twain. His escape to adventure, to the past, to humor which moves through and beyond reality, is not unlike Hemingway's escape from thinking through the simpler pleasures of wine, women, and manly exercise. Not only is Mark Twain's simple declarative style a parent of Hemingway's style; not only is his boy's-eye view of the world like Hemingway's view, like Willa Cather's, Sherwood Anderson's, even J. D. Salinger's; the publication of *The Mysterious Stranger* in 1916 reveals him mastered by the same cluster of opinions which produced the retreat to older times of Henry Adams, as well as the despair of the "lost generation" of Hemingway and Scott Fitzgerald, and the wasted land of T. S. Eliot. . . .

Clemens's Youth

One among thousands of Americans who in the early decades of the nineteenth century moved westward to seek opportunities in newly opened lands, John Marshall Clemens did not prosper in the hamlet in which his third son was born, and so, when Samuel was four years old, moved to Hannibal, a larger town with a population of almost five hundred, on the banks of the Mississippi River.

There, beside this river, Samuel Clemens grew through boyhood much as Tom Sawyer did, fascinated by the life which swarmed over its mile-wide surface or which sought refuge or sustenance on its shores. Through this frontier region passed the picturesque, sometimes mendacious or menacing, pilgrims of restlessly expanding America, up or down the river or across it toward the western plains. Young Samuel must have watched, as any boy might, admiringly, but fearfully also. He saw men maimed or killed in waterfront brawls, Negroes chained like animals for transportation to richer slave markets to the south. He had nightmares and walked in his sleep, and always remembered these things, the rude ways and tremendous talk, and the terror.

Better things were remembered also, like giant rafts and trading scows piled with produce or sweet-smelling timber, coming from or going where a boy could only guess. Gallant river steamers left wake behind in which small boys swimming or in boats could ride excitedly. Below the village lay wooded Holliday Hill, unrivaled for play at Robin Hood or pirate, and near its summit a cave tempted to exploration. Away from its boisterous riverfront, the village was "a heavenly place for a boy," he said, providing immunities and graces which he never forgot: hunting and fishing, a swimming hole, an inevitable graveyard, truant days at Glasscock's Island, and yearnings toward the better freedom of Tom Blankenship, the town drunkard's son, to whom truancy brought no penalties of conscience or recrimination. . . .

In Preparation for Huck

Given a story to tell, Clemens was almost always able to tell it well. As raconteur he had come to maturity in *Innocents Abroad*. But the invention of stories did not come easily to him. As he approached forty, he felt written out. He collected miscellaneous writings in *Sketches Old and New* and, with an eye on the market, tried to fit further adventures of the popular Colonel Sellers into a new book which failed to go well but which he published many years later, in 1891, as *The American Claimant*. He labored over a boy's story based on his early life in Hannibal, but that did not go well either.

Finally, at the suggestion of a friend, he recalled his years of steamboating and wrote, with hardly any posturing at all, of "Old Times on the Mississippi" in seven installments for the *Atlantic Monthly* in 1875. . . .

Romance of the Mississippi

On the river he became "personally and familiarly acquainted with about all the different types of human nature to be found

in fiction, biography, or history." He never read of or met any-
one again without "warm personal interest in him, for the
reason that I had known him before—met him on the river."
But for all its attention to remembered detail, "Old Times on
the Mississippi" was not in strictest sense realistic. Its narrator
seldom looked aside to notice people not admitted to the pi-
lothouse, like the sharpers, gamblers, and painted women who
plied a profitable trade on Mississippi steamers, but kept his
eyes on the river and his mind on the discipline she demanded
from men who knew her charm but also her mystery and
menace, who were skilled, not only in finding their own way
among her dangers, but in guiding others safely through.
Thus a reminiscent account becomes more than re-creation of
times that are gone and will not return because steamboating,
like the whaling of which Melville wrote in *Moby Dick*, was
the product of a way of life which was past. It speaks of appearance as opposed to reality, of innocence and experience,
of man's duty in a world of perils, and also of a conception of
the function of literature.

The Mississippi River appeared triumphantly again in *The
Adventures of Tom Sawyer* which in 1876 placed Mark Twain
once more at the head of best-seller lists. Probably no more
continuingly popular book has ever appeared in the United
States. . . .

The Reception of *Huck Finn*

Clemens established his own publishing house and launched
it in 1885 with another boy's book which he was careful to
link in the public mind to his earlier, encouragingly popular
account of young life by the Mississippi by identifying its hero
in a subtitle as "Tom Sawyer's comrade." But *The Adventures of
Huckleberry Finn* made no such immediate impression as its
predecessor. At Concord in Massachusetts, still the mecca of
genteel New England cultural aspiration, it was banished from
the local library as presenting a bad example for youth. Years

later, it was blacklisted in Denver, Omaha, and even Brooklyn. When chapters from it appeared in the *Century Magazine*, some readers found it indefensibly coarse, "destitute of a single redeeming quality."

But *The Adventures of Huckleberry Finn* has outlived almost every criticism of those who have spoken against it to become a native classic thrust forward exultantly in the face of any who still dare inquire, "Who reads an American book?"— its health endangered only by a smothering swarm of commentators who threaten to maim it with excessive kind attention. Except perhaps for *Moby Dick*, no American book has recently been opened with more tender explicatory care or by critics to whom we are better prepared to listen. . . .

Freedom and Society

The Adventures of Huckleberry Finn is the story of a boy who will not accept the kinds of freedom the world is able to offer, and so flees from them, one after another, to become to many readers a symbol of man's inevitable, restless flight. . . . It poses what has been called the inescapable dilemma of democracy—to what degree may each single and separate person live as an unencumbered individual and to what extent must he submit to distortions of personality required by society?. . .

Huckleberry Finn's solution of the problem of freedom is direct and unworldly: having tested society, he will have none of it, for civilization finally makes culprits of all men. Huck is a simple boy, with little education and great confidence in omens. One measure of his character is its proneness to deceit which, though not always successful, is instinctive, as if it were a trait shared with other wild things, relating him to nature, in opposition to the tradition-grounded, book-learned imaginative deceptions of Tom Sawyer. . . . American fictions, we are told, are filled with white boys who are influenced by darker companions.

Huck and Jim as Slaves

Huck and Jim float with their raft toward what they hope will be freedom for both. On the river or its shores many kinds of men are encountered, most of them evil or stupid or mean: cutthroats, murderers, cheats, liars, swindlers, cowards, slave hunters, dupes and hypocrites of every variety. Even the isolation from society which life on a raft might be thought to afford is violated, for malevolence also intrudes there in grotesque guises. Nor is the movement of the great brown river to be trusted. It carries Jim beyond freedom to capture again by respectable, benevolent people whose conscience is untroubled by human slavery.

The final twelve chapters take place again on land. Tom Sawyer once more appears, filled with romance-bred notions of how Jim might be freed. And Huck joins in the laborious nonsense, for he admires Tom, if he does not understand him—often on the river when confronted with crisis or cleverly, he thought, surmounting difficulties, he wished Tom had been there to aid or commend him. But the boys' make-believe at rescue becomes a travesty, for Miss Watson had granted Jim his freedom—he was no longer a slave. The narrative ends hurriedly, as if embarrassed to linger while loose ends were tied. Huck's father is dead—Jim had known that since the first stage of their journey but in kindness had withheld the knowledge. One threat to Huck's freedom is gone, but another remains, for good people again pity the brave pariah boy and offer to adopt him. But Huck will not have it: "I can't stand it," he said. "I been there before." . . .

And much has been made of the development of Huck's character, his initiation, or his disillusionment with the world and its ways, and especially the change in his attitude toward the Negro Jim whom he finally recognizes as a fellow being, more decent and honest than most of the white people who hold him and his kind in slavery.

Runaway Slaves in Sam Clemens's World

Terrell Dempsey

Terrell Dempsey, an attorney, author, and historian, lives in Hannibal, Missouri.

In the following essay, Terrell Dempsey details the racial setting of Sam Clemens's youth, giving special attention to the tragedy of runaway slaves, much of which was reported in his brother Orion's newspaper, for which Clemens worked as a reporter. Early in his life, he was witness to the horror of the runaway's prospects when he and other boys came across the mutilated body of a runaway slave in one of the inlets near an island in the Mississippi, an episode mentioned by Twain in his Autobiography. *Twain also mentions that the older brother of his friend had been providing food to the slave, who was hiding on an island. "Runaways," writes Dempsey, "were a constant feature of [Clemens's] childhood." And like Jim, what frequently motivated runaways was the wish to rejoin their families. Dempsey provides an answer to why Jim did not just go to the free state of Illinois: Slave catchers were routinely allowed to search that area.*

The year 1847 held another horror for Samuel Clemens in addition to the death of his father. In August, when the summer heat beat down on Hannibal and the temperature hovered in the upper nineties, Sam went with his playmates John Briggs and the Bowen brothers, Bart, Will, and Sam, to find refuge in the cool water of the Mississippi. They rowed out to an island for a day of swimming and fishing. They

Terrell Dempsey, "Runaway Slaves and Slave Resistance," in *Searching for Jim. Slavery in Sam Clemens's World*, Columbia, MO: University of Missouri Press, 2003, pp. 167–181. Copyright © 2003 by The Curators of the University of Missouri. All rights reserved. Reproduced by permission.

were in a slough, or channel that ran between the island and the Illinois side, when they discovered the body of a runaway slave. It must have been a frightening experience. The boys released the body from a snag, and it rose headfirst from the murky green water. The *Hannibal Journal* reported the event. "While some of our citizens were fishing a few days since on the Sny Island, they discovered in what is called Bird Slough the body of a negro man. On examination of the body, they found it to answer the description of a negro recently advertised in handbills as a runaway from Neriam Todd, of Howard County. He had on a brown jeans frock coat, homemade linen pants, and a new pair of lined and bound shoes. The body when discovered was much mutilated."

Justifying Slavery

Clemens claimed in his autobiography that Benson Blankenship, older brother of his friend, Tom, had secretly been taking food to the slave on the island, but there is no proof of that. The body of the slave, which floated up ghostlike from the river, epitomized one of the great contradictions of slavery. The slave had lost his life seeking freedom. But in Hannibal's worldview slavery was established by God for the well-being of both slave and master. Every need of the slave was met by the system. What slave in his right mind would flee?

White slave culture offered several answers to this troublesome question: Slaves were childlike creatures, easily led astray by cunning abolitionists, who tricked them into leaving the natural order of slavery. . . .

Runaways

Between 1850 and 1860, the number of slaves escaping declined nationally, while increasing in Missouri.

It is no wonder that Mark Twain's *Adventures of Huckleberry Finn* would be built around a runaway slave. Runaways were a constant feature of his childhood. Missouri slave culture even joked about them. One Marion County merchant ran an advertisement that boldly declared, "Running Away!" There followed a list of the clothing, boots, shoes, and food items he offered for sale, and he closed, "Please call before they are all run off." Runaways were an accepted topic for humor. "Darkness has fled, as the man said when his negro absconded" was a one-liner run in a local paper. The *Hannibal Journal* poked fun at a mistake in a runaway advertisement. "A Southern advertiser, describing a runaway negro, says, 'he is thirty-five feet of age!' Tall age that. That darkie was exactly six years high." Despite the jokes, running away was deadly serious business. Not only did local slaves run away to the North and East, but countless slaves from the interior of Missouri made their way toward the Mississippi or the Des Moines River. . . .

Running for freedom was no lark, yet men, women, and children risked their lives to do so. Frustrated slave catchers would kill a slave rather than let him reach freedom. The *Hannibal Journal* recorded such an incident in 1849. Two white men from Shelby County immediately to the west of Hannibal were hunting game when they saw two Negro men in a field. When the Negroes saw the white men, they fled. The whites knew immediately by their behavior that they were runaway slaves and pursued them. They stalked the slaves for several days, never able to catch them. Frustrated, when the pursuers got within rifle range, they shot one of the two runaways. They hoped that the other man would become demoralized and surrender, but he left his dying friend and ran off. The whites were distracted by the slave they had shot. This allowed his comrade to make his way to freedom. It took the wounded slave three hours to die. Rather than let him go, his pursuers preferred him dead. The value of a dead slave was no more than that of one who had escaped. However, he could still be used: His execution might serve as a warning to others.

A runaway slave in Missouri was also at risk from exposure to the elements. In the Christmas Eve edition of 1857,
the *Hannibal Messenger* reported that a female runaway slave
had frozen to death in a winter storm. Likewise, merely getting to Illinois or Iowa did not ensure freedom. The rewards
offered for captured slaves increased dramatically for those
caught outside Missouri. Slave catching in Illinois and Iowa
could be very lucrative. Upon return to his Missouri master, a
slave who was captured was sure to be whipped, jailed, and
perhaps sold. The recaptured slave's life would be hell for a
time. . . .

Appearances

The biggest obstacle to a slave was his or her physical appearance. All blacks were presumed to be slaves under Missouri
law. Therefore, any black person who was in a suspicious place
was regarded as a runaway. One very ingenious slave nearly
made his way to the Mississippi River at Hannibal with a brilliant disguise. He came from Lafayette County in the middle
of the state. As late as 1852, it was not that unusual to see an
occasional Indian in Missouri. This slave, whose name has
been lost to history, made a wig to resemble Native American
hair. He wore a turban headdress, blanket, leggings, and moc-
casins. He adorned his costume with what a Hannibal newspaper characterized as "appropriate trinkets."

The disguised slave left home on Saturday and began walking toward Hannibal. His disguise worked very well for a
time. He traveled all day Sunday. When he met up with travel-
ers who insisted on speaking with him, he faked an accent
and told them he was on his way to Hannibal to see the Indian agent to get money to return to his mountain home. He
was captured well inland of Hannibal when a Mr. Spencer,
"who is always eyeing runaways and thieves with the keenness

$500, REWARD.

Ran away from the undersigned, on Sunday the 9th inst., a negro boy named

AARON OR APE.

He is about 20 years old, six feet high, with rather unusually large legs and arms; walks bent forward with one foot turned out more than the other. I will give $150,00 reward for him if taken in the county; $100,00 reward if taken in the counties south of this and $200,00 if taken in any of the Mississippi counties or $500 if taken out of the State.

O. M. HARRIS,
Three miles south of Middddle Grove Monroe Coounty, Missouri.

REGISTER PRINT—MACON CITY, MO.

After the Fugitive Slave Act of 1850 citizens and lawmen of free states and territories were obliged, under penalty of law, to return those who had escaped from bondage back to those who considered them property. Kean Collection/Getty Images.

of a Marshal Felps [a famous Texas lawman], detected his lips as being too thick for an Indian." The bold slave was returned to his master. . . .

Separation of Families

The separation of families led slaves to run away. Sometimes they simply went to see loved ones. Other times freed slaves took great risks to liberate members of their families still in bondage. One slave was captured in Hannibal while visiting relatives. A thirty-year-old man named Milton had been sold by a Hannibal family named Dickson to another family who lived far to the south in Jefferson County. He evidently missed his own family and ran back to Hannibal to visit them. He was visiting slaves belonging to George Mahan (father of the man who would purchase Sam Clemens's boyhood home in Hannibal and open it as a museum). Milton became sick while visiting his relatives and was discovered. In his weakened state, he was easy prey for Mahan. He was captured and returned to his owner. . . .

Why Not Illinois?

Reaching Illinois did not mean freedom. Slave catchers, aware of increased rewards for Missouri slaves captured in other states, were not deterred by state borders, nor were they necessarily discouraged by the passage of time. Rewards typically increased over time. An 1853 ad offered one hundred dollars in state and two hundred dollars out. It was possible of course that abolitionists would come to the rescue of a slave captured in Illinois. When one Missouri slave girl was caught in Alton, Illinois, the abolitionists in that town raised twelve hundred dollars to purchase her from her master. Abolitionists and free blacks would often try to free slaves who had been taken into custody by law enforcement officers or slaveholders themselves. The abolitionists in Chicago could be especially aggressive. In 1854 three St. Louis slave catchers tracked a runaway slave to the windy city and met their quarry in the street. An angry free Negro intervened, and one of the slave catchers shot and wounded him. A riot almost followed. Angry Negroes surrounded the slave catchers, and the slave was spirited away. The Missourians were outraged when law enforcement officers arrived on the scene and arrested the three of them. The Missouri slave catchers were charged with assault, riot, and attempt to kidnap. The slave went free.

Jacob Sosey, editor of the *Missouri Whig*, fumed: "This is the kind of justice extended to the people of Missouri, and the slave-holding States, by the *hypocritical thieves of that mob-ruled, treason-hatching city of Chicago*. They first steal a man's property from before his eyes, and then incarcerate him in a dungeon, because he endeavored to reclaim that property peaceably." The abolitionists in Chicago could be overly vigilant. In 1857 a white Pennsylvania man, who was caring for a young black boy at the request of the boy's mother, passed through Chicago on his way to Monmouth, Illinois. Suspicious, abolitionists took the boy from him until he could prove that the child was his ward, not his slave. . . .

Runaway slaves from Hannibal were often caught just across the river, as five were in 1857, or in nearby Illinois towns, like two captured near Mendon, Illinois, in 1858. The slaves were all taken to jail. Many escaped slaves from the interior of Missouri were arrested in or near Hannibal before they could try to cross the Mississippi. A slave from Boone County was captured in Marion County in May 1842. Some— like the dead slave found by Sam Clemens and his friends in 1847, who was from Howard County—lost their gamble at the river. Both runaways had traveled nearly one hundred miles.

Social Issues in Literature

CHAPTER 2

Race in *Huck Finn*

A Blending of Black and White Voices

Shelley Fisher Fishkin

Shelley Fisher Fishkin, professor of English and director of American studies at Stanford University, has published more than forty books, including Was Huck Black? *(1993).*

In the following essay, Shelley Fisher Fishkin argues that the language of Huckleberrry Finn *indicates that Twain blended black and white personalities in the character of Huck. Twain himself claimed that his friend Tom Blankenship, the poor white son of the local drunkard, was his model for Huck, but evidence shows that Twain imbued much of the language and character of Huck with that of a ten-year-old black child named Jimmy. Twain met garrulous little Jimmy in the winter of 1871–72, wrote his wife repeated letters about him, and published an article on him in the* New York Times *in 1874, two years before he began* Adventures of Huckleberry Finn. *Not only is Huck's speech similar to Jimmy's, but so are his "topics of conversation, attitudes, limitations." They are both naïve, puzzled by the adult world, and have aversions to and nightmares about cruelty. So, in much of the story narrated by Huck, we hear the voice of Jimmy.*

Twentieth-century American criticism abounds in pronouncements about how Twain's choice of a vernacular narrator in *Huckleberry Finn* transformed modern American literature. Lionel Trilling, for example, felt that

> The prose of *Huckleberry Finn* established for written prose the virtues of American colloquial speech. . . . It has something to do with ease and freedom in the use of language.

Shelley Fisher Fishkin, "Jimmy," in *Mark Twain and African-American Voices*, Oxford, United Kingdom: Oxford University Press, 1993. Copyright © 1993 Shelley Fisher Fishkin. Reproduced by permission of Oxford University Press.

Most of all it has to do with the structure of the sentence, which is simple, direct, and fluent, maintaining the rhythm of the word-groups of speech and the intonations of the speaking voice. . . . [Twain] is the master of the style that escapes the fixity of the printed page, that sounds in our ears with the immediacy of the heard voice. . . . "As for the style of the book," Trilling concluded, "it is not less than definitive in American literature." As Louis Budd noted in 1985, "today it is standard academic wisdom that Twain's central, precedent-setting achievement is Huck's language."

A New American Voice

Before Twain wrote *Huckleberry Finn*, no American author had entrusted his narrative to the voice of a simple, untutored vernacular speaker—or, for that matter, to a child. Albert Stone has noted that "the vernacular language . . . in *Huckleberry Finn* strikes the ear with the freshness of a real boy talking out loud." Could the voice of an *actual* "real boy talking out loud" have helped Twain recognize the potential of such a voice to hold an audience's attention and to win its trust?

Twain himself noted in his autobiography that he based Huck Finn on Tom Blankenship, the poor-white son of the local drunkard whose pariah status (and exemption from school, church, etc.) made him the envy of every "respectable" boy in Hannibal. Twain wrote,

> In *Huckleberry Finn* I have drawn Tom Blankenship exactly as he was. He was ignorant, unwashed, insufficiently fed; but he had as good a heart as any boy had. His liberties were totally unrestricted. He was the only really independent person—boy or man—in the community, and by consequence he was tranquilly and continuously happy, and was envied by all the rest of us. We liked him, we enjoyed his society. And as his society was forbidden us by our parents, the prohibition trebled and quadrupled its value, and therefore we sought and got more of his society than of any other boy's.

What demands our notice is that although Tom Blankenship may have been the model for Huck's place in society, Twain never suggested that there was anything memorable about the nature of his "talk." Huck's talk, on the other hand, as many critics have noted, is the most memorable thing about him. I suggest that there was another "real boy talking out loud" whose role in the genesis of *Huckleberry Finn* has never been acknowledged.

Jimmy

On 29 November 1874, two years before he published *Tom Sawyer* or began *Adventures of Huckleberry Finn*, Mark Twain published an article called "Sociable Jimmy" in the *New York Times*. *"Sociable Jimmy" takes the place of honor as the first piece Twain published that is dominated by the voice of a child.* This fact alone would seem to mark it as deserving of scholars' attention. Strangely enough, however, it has been almost totally ignored.

In this article, Twain says he originally sent the sketch of "Jimmy" home in a letter in the days when he was a public lecturer. Although this initial letter has disappeared, subsequent letters Twain wrote home to his wife allow us to determine that the encounter he relates happened in December 1871 or January 1872, in a small town in the Midwest, probably Paris, Illinois, and that the child in question definitely existed. Twain reports that he had supper in his room, as was his habit, and that a "bright, simple, guileless little darkey boy . . . ten years old—a wide-eyed, observant little chap" was sent to wait on him. The intensity of Twain's response to the child is striking. He notes that he wrote down what the child said, and sent the record home because he

> . . . wished to preserve the memory of *the most artless, sociable, and exhaustless talker I ever came across.* He did not tell me a single remarkable thing, or one that was worth remembering; and yet he was himself so interested in his small marvels, and they flowed so naturally and comfortably from his lips, that his talk got the upper hand of my inter-

Eddie Hodges as Huck Finn in the 1960 film adaptation of the book. Grey Villet/Time Life
Pictures/Getty Images.

est, too, and *I listened as one who receives a revelation.* I took
down what he had to say, just as he said it—without alter-
ing a word or adding one.

Twain's "revelation" involved his recognition of the potential
of a "bright, simple, guileless ... wide-eyed, observant" child

as narrator. I suggest that the voice of Jimmy, the "most artless, sociable, and exhaustless talker" Twain had ever come across, became a model for the voice with which Twain would change the shape of American literature.

It was a voice that Twain contained within himself, a language and set of cadences and rhythms he could generate fluently on his own, having been exposed to many such voices in his youth. Jimmy triggered his recollection of those voices, and sparked his apprehension of the creative possibilities they entailed. We can view the remarkable impression Jimmy made upon Twain, then, as connected to Twain's awareness of the ease with which he could speak in that voice himself. As he put it in a letter to Livy [Twain's wife, Olivia] written shortly after he met Jimmy, "*I think I could swing my legs over the arms of a chair & that boy's spirit would descend upon me & enter into me.*" It was a crucial step on the road to creating Huck.

"Sociable Jimmy" consists mainly of what Twain presents as a transcription of Jimmy's engaging conversation. Twain had been intrigued for several years by the possibilities of a child as narrator, but this was the first time that he developed this perspective at any length in print. Along with "A True Story," which ran in the *Atlantic Monthly* the same month "Sociable Jimmy" ran in the *Times*, it also represented one of Twain's first extended efforts to translate African-American speech into print. Indeed, to the extent that critics took notice of the piece at all, it was as an experiment in African-American dialect. Jimmy's defining characteristic for critics seemed to be the fact that he was black. For Twain, however, Jimmy was mainly a charming and delightful *child* who captured his heart and captivated his imagination.

Dialects

In the "Explanatory" with which *Huckleberry Finn* begins, Twain enumerates seven dialects used in the book, one of which is "Missouri negro dialect." Critics have debated whether Twain did, in fact, use seven dialects, or more, or fewer; but they have generally assumed that the only "negro dialect" in the book is that spoken by African-American characters. On a phonological level, that assumption is correct: only African-American characters, for example, say "dat," as opposed to "that." But phonology alone does not describe a *voice*, as the voluminous criticism about what makes Huck's voice distinctive clearly shows. Voice involves syntax and diction, the cadences and rhythms of a speaker's sentences, the flow of the prose, the structures of the mental processes, the rapport with the audience, the characteristic stance as regards the material related.

The cadences and rhythms of Jimmy's speech, his syntax and diction, his topics of conversation, attitudes, limitations, and his ability to hold our interest and our trust bear a striking resemblance to those qualities of speech and character that we have come to identify indelibly with Huck. Both boys are naive and open, engaging and bright. They are unpretentious, uninhibited, easily impressed, and unusually loquacious. They free associate with remarkable energy and verve. And they are supremely self-confident: neither doubts for a minute that Twain (in Jimmy's case) or the reader (in Huck's) is completely absorbed by everything he has to say. I am not suggesting that Twain was being intentionally misleading either in his "Explanatory" or in his comments about the roots of Huck in Tom Blackenship: rather, I put forth the far from controversial notion that artists are notoriously unreliable critics of their own work. As I point out later on, Twain's blending of black voices with white to create the voice we know as Huck's may well have been unconscious.

Clearly, Twain is experimenting with African-American dialect in "Sociable Jimmy," just as he was in "A True Story, Repeated Word for Word as I Heard It," which appeared in the *Atlantic Monthly* the same month that "Sociable Jimmy" appeared in the *New York Times*. But although on the phono-logical level Jimmy's dialect bears some obvious resemblances to the speech of black characters in the novel, particularly Jim's, in a number of other ways his speech is closer to that of Huck. It is not just linguistically, however, that Jimmy and Huck have much in common. Even more striking than the similarities between Jimmy and Huck on the level of cadence, syntax, and diction, are the similarities between the two boys' character traits and topics of conversation.

Not Getting the Joke

The adult world remains rather confusing and cryptic to both Jimmy and Huck, who are blissfully oblivious to the gaps in their understanding. Part of the humor in both "Sociable Jimmy" and *Huckleberry Finn* stems from the reader's aware-ness that sometimes neither Jimmy nor Huck understands that a joke is being perpetrated. Twain finds Jimmy's "dense simplicity" so engaging that he devotes a bracketed aside in the piece to explicating it

> Some folks say dis town would be considerable bigger if it wa'n't on accounts of so much lan' all roun' it dat ain't got no houses on it. [This in perfect seriousness—dense sim-plicity—no idea of a joke.]

Huck, too, sometimes fails to "get" a joke. At the circus, for example, the "drunk" who had argued with the ringmaster until he gave him a chance to ride jumps on a charging horse, pulls off his outer clothes, and turns out to be one of the regular circus performers in disguise. Huck says,

> . . . then the ring-master he see how he had been fooled, and he *was* the sickest ring-master you ever see, I reckon. Why, it was one of his own men! He had got up that joke all out of his own head, and never let on to nobody. Well, I felt sheep-ish enough, to be took in so, but I wouldn't a been in that ring-master's place, not for a thousand dollars. . . .

Aversion to Cruelty

Another element Jimmy and Huck have in common is an aversion to violence and cruelty. Both boys have bad dreams about cruel and violent acts they've witnessed, and have difficulty talking about the subject. Jimmy tells us,

> I can't kill a chicken—well, I kin wring its neck off, cuz dat don't make 'em no sufferin scacely; but I can't take and chop dey heads off, like some people kin. It makes me feel so—so—well, I kin see dat chicken nights so's I can't sleep.

After the mindless killings during the feud, Huck comments:

> It made me so sick I most feel out of the tree. I ain't agoing to tell *all* that happened—it would make me sick again if I was to do that. I wish I hadn't ever come ashore that night, to see such things. I ain't ever going to get shut of them— lots of times I dream about them.

While Jimmy's comments involve chickens and Huck's involve human beings, the visceral rejection of violence and cruelty in each case is similar, as is each child's reluctance to talk about it, and the expression of personal anguish with the barely understood sleep disturbance of a child. . . .

Other Similarities

The only "real" family that each boy has is "Pa" or "Pap" and in both cases the father has a history of alcohol problems that both children describe with unembarrassed frankness. In both cases (despite Jimmy's assertion that Pa's drinking days are over), the problem is ongoing.

Jimmy and Huck also share some matters of taste: each boy is especially awed by a particular clock, and both set themselves up as judges of refinement. Jimmy and Huck are both easily impressed by other things as well—Jimmy by the size of the church steeple and the weather vane at its top, Huck by the Grangerfords' fake plaster fruits and Emmeline's dreadful poetry.

Finally, Jimmy and Huck are both at home with dead animals—dead cats, dead fish. These are simply a part of their world and they wouldn't dream of omitting them from their chatty conversation. They bring them in casually and comfortably, unaware that details about the dead animal might disrupt their listener's equilibrium or digestion. Jimmy entertains Twain at dinner, apropos of nothing in particular, with an anecdote about the dead cat in the well that supplied Twain's drinking water:

> Bill's down on cats. So is de gals—waiter gals. When dey ketches a cat bummin' aroun' heah, dey jis' *scoops* him— 'deed dey do. Dey snake him into de cistern—dey's been cats drownded in dat water dat's in yo' pitcher. I seed a cat in dare yistiddy—all swelled up like a pudd'n. I bet you dem gals done dat.

With similarly jarring candor, Huck fails to edit out of his lyrical description of dawn on the river a decidedly pungent dead fish:

> then the nice breeze springs up, and comes fanning you from over there, so cool and fresh, and sweet to smell, on account of the woods and the flowers; but sometimes not that way, because they've left dead fish laying around, gars [an inedible predatory fish], and such, and they do get pretty rank . . .

Perhaps Jimmy's sociable chatter about the dead cats remained in Twain's subconscious, when, a few years after his encounter with Jimmy, he introduced Huck Finn to the world in *Tom Sawyer* carrying a dead cat.

Tom hailed the romantic outcast:

"Hello, Huckleberry!"

"Hello yourself, and see how you like it."

"What's that you got?"

"Dead Cat."

Dead cats enter the scene in *Huckleberry Finn* as well, this time *en masse*, when the Bricksville crowd is gunning for the king and the duke at their third performance of "The Royal Nonesuch." Huck says,

> If I know the signs of a dead cat being around, and I bet I do, there was sixty-four of them went in.

Both Jimmy and Huck are proud that they "know the signs of a dead cat being around" and are only too glad to share their knowledge.

Twain had long admired the artful presentation of many of those qualities Jimmy so fully embodied. For example, referring to a story James Whitcomb Riley told, Twain commented,

> The simplicity and innocence and unconsciousness of the old farmer are perfectly simulated, and the result is a performance which is thoroughly charming and delicious. This is art—and fine and beautiful.

If "simplicity and innocence and unconsciousness" are to be desired, who better to embody these traits than a child?

"Sociable Jimmy" was Twain's first published work in which the voice of a child took center stage. In the years that immediately followed its publication, Twain became increasingly aware of the distinctive possibilities of the choice of a child narrator. As he once put it, "Experience has taught me long ago that if ever *I* tell a boy's story . . . it is never worth printing. . . . To be successful and worth printing, the imagined boy would have to tell the story *himself* and let me act merely as his amanuensis [secretary]." That was, of course, precisely the role in which Twain placed himself as he copied down Jimmy's speech that evening. It is the same role Twain assumed in his imagination when he began writing *Huckleberry Finn*. In the recently discovered manuscript of the beginning of the novel, Huck's opening lines, "You don't know about me . . ." are preceded by the words,

Huckleberry Finn

reported by Mark Twain.

"All Right, Then, I'll Go to Hell"

Jonathan Arac

Jonathan Arac, Mellon Professor of English at the University of Pittsburgh, is the author of Emergence of American Literary Narrative, 1820–1860 *and* Critical Genealogies.

In the following essay, Jonathan Arac's aim is to view Twain's artistic choices within the context of the novel's setting and publication. Twain's story ignores much of the complexity of racial issues, according to Arac. The citizens of the southern and central states were not uniformly in favor of slavery. In his tale, Twain never acknowledges that many Americans, including some southerners, regarded the Declaration of Independence as a document that protected black people as well as white. Twain shows Huck struggling without assistance, finding, according to Arac, no fellow citizens and no egalitarian national philosophy to support him, when in fact, this would not have been the case. Twain focuses on the moral and religious dilemma without regard to the country's struggles with itself.

I prefer to understand *Huckleberry Finn* as built from highly selective artistic choices rather than simple reflections of the reality of antebellum [pre–Civil War] America. To gauge Twain's choices requires going behind his own historical claims and memories and placing them in the context of a fuller range of materials. In his evocation of the solid slaveholding ideology and practices of his childhood, Twain makes things much simpler than they were either in his own life or in the life of the United States.

Jonathan Arac, "'All Right, Then, I'll Go to Hell,'" in *"Huckleberry Finn" as Idol and Target*, Madison: University of Wisconsin Press, 1997, pp. 37–62. Copyright © 1997 by the Board of Regents of the University of Wisconsin System. Reproduced by permission.

The Setting of *Huckleberry Finn*

Sam Clemens was born to a family that owned enslaved African Americans, and he was born at a time that marked an important change in the history of slavery in the United States. The commitment to slavery hardened as the profitability of slave labor increased and opposition to slavery became correspondingly more vehement. In the 1830s, the great boom in cotton that was opening the lands of the "South-West" made human property increasingly more valuable and provided a motive for the original slaveholding states to preserve their commitment to this system. Moreover, many of those who came west to settle Missouri pushed on that far, rather than stopping in southern Indiana or Illinois, precisely because they wanted either to keep or to acquire slaves. South Carolina's attempt to "nullify" federal tariffs set forward the kinds of argument that would eventually be used on behalf of secession. . . . And in the North, the 1830s were notable for mob violence against abolitionists, led not by people like Huck's pap but by "gentlemen of property and standing." In the wake of the mob murder of the abolitionist editor Elijah Lovejoy at Alton, Illinois, in 1837, Abraham Lincoln devoted his first memorable speech, in 1838, to the problems caused by mobs and "increasing disregard for law." With his constant concern for the state of feeling as fundamental to social and political life, Lincoln warned that "by the operation of *this mobocratic spirit* . . . the strongest bulwark of any Government . . . may effectually be broken down . . . I mean the *attachment* of the People." Against this tendency, Lincoln urged that "reverence for the laws . . . become the *political religion* of the nation". All of this supports Twain's notebook memory of the "sacredness" of slave property.

Nonetheless, even after the 1830s, through the slaveholding states there was more dissent than Twain's notebook account allows for. . . .

The most important modern histories of slavery in the United States find it important to mention that there were indeed a "few white Southerners" who "gave sanctuary to fugitives or directed them along their routes", despite the financial incentive offered in every slave state by laws that "required the owner of a fugitive to compensate the captor for his trouble". Eugene Genovese summarizes from a body of legal materials and earlier monographs: "Some of the slaves who ran away ran to other white people. In scattered cases they ran to whites who could help them escape. A few white men protected runaway slaves at great personal risk," although a few were "less altruistic" and "took in runaways to ease their own labor shortage." . . .

Models for Huck

It is well known that Tom Blankenship, son of the town drunk in Hannibal, provided a major model for the figure of Huck Finn: "He had as good a heart as any boy ever had. His liberties were totally unrestricted. He was the only really independent person—boy or man—in the community, and by consequence was tranquilly and continuously happy, and was envied by all the rest of us" (Twain, *Autobiography*). It is not so commonly known, although it has been in circulation since Albert Bigelow Paine's 1912 authorized biography, presumably as an oral account from Twain to Paine, that Tom's older brother Ben Blankenship provided a model for assisting a fugitive slave. According to Paine, this experience of Ben's "provided Mark Twain with that immortal episode in the story of Huckleberry Finn—the sheltering of Nigger Jim." . . .

Society vs. Heart

Paine contrasts Ben's experience with "Huck's struggle." Paine sees Huck as caught "between conscience and the law," but the point of chapter 31 is that conscience and the law are wholly in accord with one another. The law of slavery works together with what Twain, in a famous comment, called Huck's "deformed conscience." They both oppose what Paine's account calls "human sympathy" and what Twain called Huck's "sound heart". Paine has restored *conscience* to its conventional position as a transcendent arbiter of morality, and has placed *law* as its opponent, standing for the socially conditioned, historically limited views of slaveholding society. But in chapter 31, law is never even mentioned, only religion and social pressure.

Ben Blankenship was an important human example of secret action, but part of Twain's claim in the notebook reminiscence is that there was no public, articulated ideological support for opposition to slavery. . . .

Church and Country

Besides the language of damnation that preoccupies Huck in chapter 31, Christianity also includes a language of love. Huck has early in the book been told about praying for "spiritual gifts": "I must help other people, and do everything I could for other people, and look out for them all the time, and never think about myself". But he "couldn't see no advantage about it" and so puts it from mind. Yet it is just such Sunday school altruism in this sequence for Huck to sacrifice his own salvation so as to save Jim. So, too, the United States was not only a slaveholding society but also a society founded on principles of liberty and independence. Although the discourse of civic equality among slaveholders was always apt ground for ironists, it did provide an alternative, culturally authoritative resource, with which even Southerners might—and some did—argue against slavery. Twain steers as clear as he can of this language. The season was right for it—Huck and Jim come off Jackson's Island on the June rises, and Twain even proposed in his notes for the book that Huck run into a Fourth of July speech. But the "Declaration of Independence" is mentioned only in Huck's comically confused characterization of the antics of Henry VIII, and the only person in the book to use the language of "rights" is pap in his poisonous claims that his rights are violated by a "govment" that lets a man of color vote. . . .

In the time that *Huckleberry Finn* was being written, the principle that "all men are created equal" was being written out of the national consensus; the United States, having quashed the Southern rebellion, was rapidly distancing itself from revolutionary principles and sympathies. . . .

In a Religious Wilderness

Huck's "crisis" is like that of a Christian in the wilderness, not like that of a citizen in debate; his moment of judgment is not a courtroom scene, and even his anxieties about stealing someone else's slave never involve legal penalties, only damnation and social ostracism. Twain excludes the category of law because even in the debased form of slave law, the law rests on a claim to justice, and the notion of justice is a culturally valued abstraction that could support Huck in his moment of need, just as earlier Judge Thatcher offered the legal form to protect Huck's money from Pap.

I have argued that to keep pure a reader's sense of Huck's individual autonomy, Twain had to purge from Huck's consciousness the available alternative languages of value in post-Jacksonian America. Since, as I have shown, these languages figure in the book, however minimally, it was indeed Twain's artistic choice to exclude them from this scene. This is an honorable and powerful literary strategy, but its effect is to disconnect Huck not only from his own time, but also from the time Twain was writing in, for these discourses still carried considerable weight in Twain's 1880s. The effect now of idolizing a passage that depends on such a technique is to remove consideration of *Huckleberry Finn* from the actualities of our time too. . . .

Property and Race

Jocelyn Chadwick-Joshua

Jocelyn Chadwick-Joshua was director of the American Studies program at the Dallas Institute for the Humanities when the following viewpoint was written.

In an answer to critics who say the novel is racist, Jocelyn Chadwick-Joshua writes that Huckleberry Finn *is just the opposite: an attack on racism. For example, Jim continues to rise in Huck's eyes as he gives evidence of not being a stereotype but of having intelligence and heart. Huck, having always been an outsider but nonetheless indoctrinated by the slaveholding society, is neither a slaver nor an abolitionist. So, despite his sympathy for Jim, he is shocked by the idea of "stealing" Miss Watson's property. The growing closeness between the two men is illustrated by black Jim's open confessions about his family to a white boy. Huck sees Jim as an ally against the two white rascals who come to invade their lives. Twain intensifies black fear through a scene of white townspeople threatening to lynch Sherburn. All the whites join the mob, while the blacks hide. The argument ends with Huck's profound decision to help free Jim, even if it means he will go to hell.*

*A*dventures of Huckleberry Finn presents African American readers with . . . a series of dilemmas. The alleged (re)invisibility of Jim creates in the novel's midsection another set of issues for the African American reading audience and others who identify with the "problem" of race. . . .

Jim Changes in Huck's Eyes

As Huck could not, neither can we simply jump arbitrarily from his discovery of Jim as a regular, visible human being in

Jocelyn Chadwick-Joshua, "In the Dark Southern Fashion: Encounters with Society," in *The Jim Dilemma: Reading Race in "Huckleberry Finn,"* Jackson: University Press of Mississippi, Jackson, 1978, pp. 61–114. Copyright © 1978 by University Press of Mississippi. All rights reserved. Reproduced by permission.

the novel's first section to his truly profound assertion at the conclusion of the midsection when he decides to continue to protect Jim: "All right, then, I'll *go* to hell". How does Huck come to consciously yield up his soul for his changed belief? To grow with Huck, we must understand his affection and his nineteenth-century sense of loyalty and moral rightness and, more importantly, his unwavering, consistent, indomitable respect for Jim as a human being, a man, a mentor whose voice must ultimately supersede the voices of the widow, Miss Watson, Judge Thatcher, and the whole South. For a real transformation to take place, Huck's allegiance to Jim must develop to the degree that he feels compelled to act. Through powerfully provocative maneuvers, Twain moves us to consider the ways Jim is constantly recruiting Huck's support and solidifying his subsequent transformation, thereby sustaining and expanding Jim's only chance for freedom. . . .

Huck's Awakening

The physical and vocal juxtaposition Twain establishes here between Huck and Jim is critical in that Jim completely understands the tenuousness of his position of slavery/freedom; Huck is beginning to understand the extent of a commitment, a commitment that stands in direct contradiction to what he has been taught, has observed, and has believed. Huck at this point has trouble accepting such a commitment. By placing the characters in such distinctive, contrastive positions, Twain engages the audience in complementary psychological aspects of the Jim dilemma. The reader identifies not with Jim alone or with Huck but with each representative mental attitude simultaneously. Whether we agree or disagree with Huck or Jim, Twain thrusts us into their world. If we align ourselves with Huck's awakening, we question many of our own social premises about property and authority. . . .

Huck's Racial Dilemma

Huck's thinking shifts from the naively innocent racist point of view in the first third of the novel. The microcosmic voice of the slaveholding South becomes more prominent in his internal dialogue as he accepts an increasing degree of involvement in Jim's situation:

> I tried to make out to myself that *I* warn't to blame, because *I* didn't run Jim off from his rightful owner; but it warn't no use, conscience up and says, every time, "But you knowed he was running for his freedom, and you could a paddled ashore and told somebody." . . . Conscience says to me, "What had poor Miss Watson done to you, that you could see her nigger go off right under your eyes and never say one single word? What did that poor old woman do to you, that you could treat her so mean? Why, she tried to learn you your book, she tried to learn you your manners, she tried to be good to you every way she knowed how. *That's* what she done."

Indeed, what a way to treat a poor, old woman who, though she traffics in human beings—buying, selling, and separating families—represents the emblem of Christian love and veracity with which Huck is all too familiar.

Twain through the art of his satire has made the ugly seem so palatable that the reader along with Huck momentarily forgets his position before revolting from it. Huck needs more time to assimilate all that is happening to him if his transformation is to be authentic, substantive, and complete. Such slow discovery seems a luxury with which the modern audience, particularly those who find the novel racist, is impatient. Opponents would have us believe that Huck's psychological and moral dilemma is simple avoidance. The text does not support that position, however. It should not be lightly dismissed that Huck wishes he were dead, for death would obviate the need to make the decision facing him between socially endorsed racism and ostracized humanity. A solution favoring either Jim or Miss Watson would require that he reject inculcated pretruths, or idols, or newly evolving truths. . . .

Jim Confides in Huck

Jim's continued verbalization of his dream heightens Huck's apprehension, particularly when Jim shatters the central myth that the slave family did not truly experience filial affection, responsibility, and duty. He reveals to Huck his plan first to purchase his wife, who is on another plantation, and then to work together with her to purchase their children. What chills—freezes—Huck's body and soul is Jim's implacable resolve to procure an "Ab'litionist to go and steal them" if the masters refuse to sell. This voice expands the voice on Jackson's Island into a voice of decisive action and strategy. The fascinating irony here lies with Huck Finn's "astonishment" and deduction that Jim has just developed these yearnings and this voice. Huck is actually speaking for post-Reconstruction readers who do not feel the same intensity over slavery that antebellum [pre–Civil War] and Reconstruction social thinkers felt. In truth, Jim allows this outburst of rebellious sentiments here because he feels safe with Huck and because, perhaps for the first time in his life, freedom is within reach. Jim has always wanted his family back, whole, as Twain later reveals more clearly; only now does he express the idea to a white. . . .

Neither Slaver nor Abolitionist

Jim is an African American man who, after some reticence on the island, decides to trust the white boy. This white boy has his own plan for escape and is not an abolitionist. No one has to tell Jim Huck's position on the slavery issue. A consistent diet of revelation and persuasion anchored in reassurance is necessary, for he knows they will encounter other influences along the journey to freedom. Masterfully, Jim succeeds in conveying his sincere love and gratitude to Huck, once again placing on Huck's heart and conscience, and on the reader's conscience, the import of the relationship they have thus far forged together. Huck is the friend, the only friend, the only white friend Jim has ever had. He is also the passport, the only one who can give Jim what he now needs, his access to freedom. Jim ensures that no matter whom Huck meets or what social circumstances he might encounter, he will feel his singularity as an actor outside of—and above—his real class allegiance as construed by the slaveholding society. When he meets the two bounty hunters, for example, Huck shows the result of this development. His trying to tell the "truth" about Jim's ethnicity fails, and he transforms Jim not only into a white man but into Pap-Jim Finn. Huck, responding sublimi-nally to Jim's parting words, constructs an intricate lie on a lie. He "promises" the hunters, "I won't let no runaway niggers get by me if I can help it". . . .

Dangers for the Runaway

The elaborate satirical discussion on just how to restrain Jim reveals the seriousness and the earnestness of the king's and duke's lack of respect and simple humanity toward Jim. Al-though a painful spectacle, it foreshadows Chapter 31 and contrasts Huck's concern for Jim with the way the king and duke perceive him as other, or as [critic] David Smith re-marks, "object". Although Huck and Jim can identify and em-pathize, initially, with the sufferings and injustices done to the king and duke, the reverse is not true. The two "royals" em-body the frequent sentiment of those in the (un)reconstructed South that no one suffered as they had been made to suffer. The duke succinctly articulates this view when he has been bested by the king in a struggle over who will sleep in which bed: "'Tis my fate to be always ground into the mire under the iron heel of oppression. Misfortune has broken my once haughty spirit; I yield, I submit; 'tis my fate. I am alone in the world—let me suffer; I can bear it". When we juxtapose this over-acted scene with the true adversities of not only the

Film still from the 1960 movie adaptation of Huckleberry Finn *with Eddie Hodges as Huck and Archie Moore as Jim. Huck's position on the slavery issue is being questioned. He is neither a slaver nor an abolitionist. As his character develops he looks deeply for answers.* MGM/The Kobal Collection.

slaves thus far encountered but the dangers surrounding all African Americans in the book, such as the professor from the North, we see satire at its most acute. These sleazy hustlers, of course, do not know what real spiritual suffering means: to yield self and dignity to fellow humans who view you as nothing more than chattel [property].

Lynching

The succeeding episodes allow Huck to encounter other, apparently peripheral southern African Americans. When Huck witnesses Sherburn's cold-blooded killing of "the best-naturedest old fool in Arkansaw," Boggs, he also witnesses something of equal importance—the attempted lynching of Sherburn and the reaction to this impending action by the southern slaves. Chapter 22 begins with Huck's describing the slaves and the growing lynch mob: "They swarmed up the street towards Sherburn's house, a-whooping and yelling and raging like Injuns, and everything had to clear the way or get run over and tromped to mush, and it was awful to see." . . .

The slaves, unlike the whites, cannot come to the fore to observe the mob solely for the taste of spectacle. They observe, as they must, to know what is developing around them. That they and only they in Twain's version "break and skaddle back out of reach" with alacrity as the mob approaches them shows their awareness of the immediate danger. The tenacity and blood lust of the mob creates an indisputable difference between the two groups. We see this scene in full color, color articulated in southern terms. Erasing the race factor diminishes and cheapens the role of blacks in the novel. Whites have no reason to run from this lynch mob. . . .

Jim's Manhood

Juxtaposed to the depiction of lynching is Huck's revelatory personal insight, in Chapter 23, that Jim cared just as much for his people as white people do for theirs. Huck hears Jim moaning and mourning to himself, when Jim thinks Huck is asleep. The reader remembers those early verbal battles between Jim and Huck about family, harems, boarding houses, and wisdom. Although they may have seemed humorous but perhaps not vital to plot development, those discussions and others in the novel's first third have prepared the reader for what transpires here. Huck, a product of his environment, could not initially identify Jim as a loving, caring husband and father. But now, in a major turning point in the novel, he sees a father who is most contrite for his mistakes.

Twain elevates Jim to a stature in this chapter unparalleled by any characters yet introduced. Notably, he does so just after Colonel Sherburn's extended definition on what makes a man. In one crystalline moment, Jim's manhood emerges. Here is a man who has undertaken the most dangerous quest possible for a southern African American in the nineteenth century. Here is a man who can show emotion over the loss of his family. Here is a man who shares with his friend a dark truth about himself as a father. . . .

Despite the fact that Jim expresses himself with "substandard" English, despite having boxed 'Lizabeth's ears, despite having been on a raft with two rogues who have reenslaved him, Jim transcends his marginality; he is much more than "half-a-man." He is above the South. Huck can now make his affirming statement that Jim must care for his family as much as white people do for theirs: not a racist statement, as opponents of the book have alleged, but rather a racial awakening by Huck as Jim eclipses Huck's own Pap. It is a statement that denies one of the ugliest and most pervasive and pernicious stereotypes encouraged by slavemasters. . . .

Clemens's Observations

We cannot be certain that Twain ever experienced an auction while growing up, but he did have an occasion to see slaves being moved to auction: "I have no recollection of ever seeing a slave auction in that town; but I am suspicious that that is because the thing was a common and commonplace spectacle, not an uncommon and impressive one. I vividly remember seeing a dozen black men and women chained to one another, once, and lying in a group on the pavement, awaiting shipment to the Southern slave market. Those were the saddest faces I have ever seen. Chained slaves could not have been a common sight or this picture would not have made so strong and lasting an impression upon me". That strong impression on Huck—and Twain—comes to a crucial juncture in Chapter 31. Most important here is that the feeling of love between blacks and whites show Huck's readiness to move to action. . . .

Huck's Soul Sacrifice

Once again Huck must take time to deliberate his actively working to free a runaway slave, just as earlier it had taken him fifteen minutes to decide to break another social taboo by humbling himself to a nigger. The mental battle is not easily won. Huck naturally falls back on his previous training from Miss Watson and the widow. But when that training does not help him make up his mind, he prays for guidance, only then realizing the falsity and emptiness of the guidance he thinks he seeks. As he remembers his experiences with Jim, the true meaning of Christian faith, loyalty, and love emerge. . . .

> I was a trembling, because I'd got to decide, forever, betwixt two things, and I knowed it. I studied a minute, sort of holding my breath, and then says to myself:
>
> "All right, then, I'll *go* to hell"—and tore it up.

The midsection of the novel concludes with this cosmic reversal. A linguistic irony deposes southern heritage and its dislocated piety in favor of an ideal arising solely from the black slave's action—his proof of himself as a whole man. Huck decides to act, a decision that in his mind damns his soul to everlasting hellfire. Talking with students around the country, I find it necessary to explain the significance and lasting impact that language held for the nineteenth century. Today's youth—and some adults as well—see language as something impermanent and temporal. They can say whatever they want and think nothing of the consequences or the effects of frivolous usage on their audience. But Huck's line, "All right, then, I'll *go* to hell," is completely earnest. Think, I ask audiences of all ages and ethnicities, really think about a literal heaven and a literal hell. Whether they are believers or not, Huck is, and we must view this scene from his perspective. There is no reprieve, no appeal from hell; once in, one is there forever, for eternity, and forever is a long time.

Given the scope of this decision, for whom or for what would they be willing to go to hell, I then ask students. Just as they could not say that they would follow the example of the free northern professor, who goes South and meets Pap Finn on the main street, most have no answer for this question, given Huck's parameters. Until readers examine this section carefully and acknowledge Huck's dilemma from his perspective, the tremendous sacrifice of this scene is lost, and so is its triumph. Not only are they lost in this scene but in its parallel scenes in Chapters 40 and 42, in which Jim must answer "What price freedom?" Few critics have addressed these scenes as parallel, but the continuity is clear. Huck makes a focused decision to sacrifice his eternal Soul, thereby responding to the question of the cost of freedom. Jim, too, must confront this dilemma. Like Huck, he will ultimately place his desire for freedom below the safety of another human being, in this case Tom Sawyer. What price freedom for Jim? His sacrifice so that Tom Sawyer stays alive. What a model for us, all of us, black or white.

The Inversion of Black and White

Carl F. Wieck

Carl F. Wieck is senior lecturer in English at the University of Tampere, Finland. He is the author of Refiguring "Huckleberry Finn" *and* Lincoln's Quest for Equality.

The thesis of Carl F. Wieck's article is the inversion of black and white in Mark Twain's novel, as revealed by his ironic narrator who has been steeped in the demeaning Southern stereotypes of blacks. Such attitudes include the view that white means goodness and intelligence and black means ignorance and malevolence. Yet Jim and other blacks are portrayed here as cunning, smart, and kind, whereas whites are portrayed as gullible and cruel. The symbol of a diseased white attitude is Huck's father, pap, described as "white to make a body sick." The contrast between Tom Sawyer and black Jim in the last evasion section underscores the contradiction of the Southern view. Wieck argues that most readers never understand the irony of the point of view through which Twain portrays society and race as it really was.

When late in Mark Twain's *Adventures of Huckleberry Finn* Huck says of Jim, "I knowed he was white inside", it requires no effort to accept this statement as an innocent expression of approval of the Southern way of life by an ignorant fourteen-year-old boy (What is "white" is taken by that boy to be good, proper, and right but is contradicted by Jim's black skin, which, according to the teachings of Huck's society, should enclose completely opposite, "black" qualities. Huck's words, however, can be considered pivotal to attempting a deeper analysis of the position of blacks and whites in Twain's novel, since inversion of roles and values lies at the heart of the author's ironic and subversive approach to his subject. Early in the book, Twain wastes no time in beginning to display whites in a negative light while conversely showing blacks to be possessed of the very qualities that the whites consider to be the prerogative of their color only.)

Reversing Black and White

Our first encounter with Jim—a man possessing no last name, as was commonly the case, and who is hence easily seen as a rootless black Everyman—finds Tom Sawyer exploiting him for some cheap "fun." Tom settles for hanging Jim's hat from a tree limb, but only after Huck opposes the more radical measure of tying Jim himself to a tree. Tom sees Jim more as a plaything than as a human being with rights equal to his own, while Huck only backs away from Tom's original scheme for the selfish reason that Jim "might wake and make a disturbance, and then they'd find out I warn't in" At the very least, then, the white boys' treatment of the black man must be seen as insensitive, since Jim would not have been likely to share in the "fun" of such an action. Tom and Huck have *their* fun when Jim turns the experience into a story about having been ridden around the world by witches, but it is Jim who has the last laugh when he uses the tale, together with the "five-center piece" left behind by Tom as payment for candles, to make profit from curious fellow slaves. The talent of the black man in this instance far outshines the actions of the white boys. . . .

White in the Negative

Twain again contrasts white with black in describing pap. The fifty year old has no gray in his hair to indicate a mellowing with age but possesses "all black" hair that is "long and tangled and greasy". Pap's "long, mixed up whiskers" are of the same hue, which produces a dramatic contrast with the color of his face. As Huck describes it, ("There warn't no color in his face, where his face showed; it was white; not like another man's white, but a white to make a body sick, a white to make a body's flesh crawl—a tree-toad white, a fish-belly white".) This depiction leads us to understand the strange fact that there can actually be negative white (or, in this case, the absence of color altogether), and, from what we later learn of pap and his values, there is little question but that symbolic importance is linked to this perception. The description of pap's hair and his "fish-belly white" complexion also creates a picture of the kind of dead body the river might wash up, and when his corpse does drift by in a floating house, it is, significantly, naked, albeit dry. The antiblack stance exhibited by pap in the novel can, moreover, be viewed as placing him unequivocally at the extreme "white" end of any color scale, since no shadings can be distinguished in the opinions he expresses. . . .

Black in the Positive

Twain no doubt enjoys his gentle joke at the expense of the virulently prejudiced, white pap. It meshes neatly with an overall strategy designed to regularly tweak the nose of pat prejudice through making black "white." As might be expected, Jim is the most visible beneficiary of this approach, and we repeatedly find him exhibiting positive qualities and emotions. In addition to being intelligent, this runaway slave is seen as generous, humane, clever, perceptive, faithful, and self-sacrificing, to mention but a few of the "white" features assigned to him. More than once we observe him stand Huck's watch on the raft when the boy is tired, and Huck also informs us, with the offensive if not fully realized condescension that Twain knew to be characteristic of even well-meaning Southerners, that "Jim had a wonderful level head, for a nigger: he could most always start a good plan when you wanted one". It is Jim who knows about "signs" and who has the practical abilities that contribute so much to making the raft more livable and effective as a "home." The first time Huck can bring himself to call Jim "white," however, it is only with great hesitation and under outside pressure from two slave catchers. Twain nevertheless allows Huck to slowly distance himself from pap's narrow views and grow close enough to Jim so that by the late stages of the book the boy *"knowed"* Jim "was white inside" (emphasis added).

This development progresses by fits and starts, as with any human relationship, and we more than once see Huck frustrated in his discussions with Jim at what he views as "nigger" obtuseness. In every case Twain has Jim win the argument and defeat Huck by using a logic that is highly effective in spite of not corresponding to the usual "white" pattern. Huck is also troubled by his companion's seeming lack of respect for prevailing laws concerning family members of slaves. Blinded by standard Southern biases, Huck overlooks the crucial fact that Jim's plan for freeing his family calls for him to respect existing laws if at all possible and to resort to the sweat of his brow before having recourse to less legal action. Thus, despite the frequent application to Jim of the demeaning term "nigger" by all and sundry, he is never seen by the reader to be anything less than decent, kind, and tolerant. In Huck's deepest soul searching the boy must also finally admit that "somehow I couldn't seem to strike no places to harden me against him, but only the other kind". . . .

Exploiting Jim

During the Evasion section of the novel Jim is exploited by Tom for the selfish purposes of Tom's "adventure." While Jim goes along with the game as best he can, Twain allows us to understand that although the town gossips consider the evidence discovered after the Evasion proves that "the nigger's crazy", every one of the details mentioned actually had Tom at its source. The Evasion is thus used in a humorous fashion, but all its features point to a crazed white world where nor-

Film still from the 1960 film version of Huckleberry Finn. *Huck recognizes Jim's practical abilities and contributions and views him as "white inside."* MGM/The Kobal Collection.

mal logic is discounted, where a black human being who would sacrifice his own freedom in order to save a young white boy who has treated him as a plaything is regarded by the white community as deserving to be lynched. It is clearly not black values that are insane here.

When Jim is recaptured and returned to his cabin prison after nursing the wounded Tom, the ability of the Southern white world to protect even a recognized black hero is seen to be insubstantial at best. The doctor's intervention on Jim's behalf eliminates only the cussing, while Huck's well-meant but all too painfully silent hopes for better treatment for his friend prove useless and, as might be expected, go unfulfilled: Jim, who, as we learn later, is actually legally free at this point, remains, literally and figuratively, heavily chained. Twain's unusually heavy-handed satire at the expense of even well-meaning pre– as well as post–Civil War Southern whites can, it appears, only be ignored by a conscious effort on the part of the reader. The black man shows uncommon bravery, whereas whites at every level prove ineffectual at providing even minimal recognition or recompense for the accomplishment of a "white" ideal. Twain once again gives us a "nigger" who is "white" to compare with "gentlemen" who are "black." . . .

Although Huck, because of his upbringing by pap and the white Southern world, is astonished to learn that Jim seemed to "care just as much for his people as white folks does for theirn", Jim proves himself at every turn worthy of Huck's view of him as "white inside," while that judgment would fit few of the white characters in the novel. . . .

As a reconstructed Southerner living in the North, Twain evidently felt that the South had to be seen from the eyes of a Southerner if the inconsistencies it embodied were to be most fully exposed. Huck, therefore, is his instrument for prying open the door of years of ignorance, prejudice, and hypocrisy. And Huck's protective, chameleon-like cloak of invisibility is created not only by being one of "them" and employing "their" language, including the word "nigger," but also by the fact that he is slowly being educated as he experiences various facets of life in the pre-Civil War South. Twain, in this manner, initiates Huck and the reader simultaneously into the mysteries of the black-white dilemma and the savagery of uncivilized "sivilized" Southern society. . . .

The World as It Is

The inversion of black and white is not, therefore, a simple equation or a neatly predictable feature of *Huckleberry Finn*. There are, as well, several instances where a reader might take offense by not stopping to consider that Twain was showing a world as it existed, warts and all, that that world was one where blacks were considered subhuman, and that "nigger" was the most commonly used epithet, especially among the lowest classes, who had the most to fear from the possible rise of that two-legged "property." Hence, it should not strike us as out of place or improper to find the minstrel-show approach exploited for humorous ends in connection with Jim (as is well known, Twain had a predilection for minstrel shows and mourned their passing). However, as Kenny J. Williams points out, "No matter how foolish Jim may appear and despite the number of times he is called 'nigger,' in the final analysis he cannot be burlesqued. But the fact that he is not absolutely part of that happy lot of plantation slaves who people American literature is lost on those who reduce the novel to an exercise in name-calling." . . .

Stereotyping

For those who would nonetheless see Twain as having written a racist novel on the grounds that the word "nigger" appears in its pages and that there is laughter at the expense of some of those "niggers," it may perhaps prove instructive to consider the following facts concerning what the author does *not* include in his work. At no point in the novel does he resort to stereotypical physical descriptions of blacks. Although Jim is given "hairy arms and breast," and Nat's face is described as "good-natured and chuckle-headed" with his smile rendered in the manner mentioned above, we never see any black person in the book endowed with thick lips or the kind of mouth frequently overemphasized in minstrel shows. There are no rolling eyes or flared nostrils, and at no point do Negroid features of any kind find a place within the text of Twain's book. Blacks in the novel are never referred to in any of the demeaning ways all too often resorted to, they are never indicated to be mentally deficient, nor do we find flip comparisons to apes, monkeys, or other animals. . . .

Twain's Intent

It would therefore appear that Mark Twain wished to write a novel in support of the free black in the post-Reconstruction

South. . . . As [critic] Richard K. Barksdale observes: "If the ironic statement made by an author in a work of fiction is too subtly wrought, it will not be effectively communicated to the average reader. The continuing controversy about *Adventures of Huckleberry Finn* suggests that the American reading public, in the main, has never fully understood the author's ironic message."

A Racist Civilization vs. Freedom

David E.E. Sloane

David E.E. Sloane, professor of English at the University of New Haven, in Connecticut, has written on Mark Twain and Thomas Edison, among others. He is the author of Student Companion to Mark Twain *and "Sister Carrie," Theodore Dreiser's Sociological Tragedy.*

In the following essay, David E.E. Sloane discusses how Huck and Jim both escape civilization to a state of nature on a deserted island in the Mississippi River. Isolated here, both white boy and black man are drawn together in trust. The two runaways, (one reborn after faking his own death,) become partners. Jim has the courage to confide to Huck that he is running away and will even use the help of abolitionists to free his wife and children. Although Huck has escaped civilization, he has not shed its tenets. Only later will he decide to be ruled by his heart instead of society's conscience. On their journey, Jim speaks of himself as property but realizes jubilantly that, having run away, he now owns himself. Huck's maturation is seen in his relationship to Jim: his two cruel practical jokes are proof of his boyishness. As he abandons this behavior, he grows up. The island section ends with Huck's famous line, "They're after us!"—not me, not you, but "us."

Huck's escape from Pap and "sivilization" initiates his meeting and joining with Jim on Jackson's Island. The Jackson Island interlude establishes trust between the two fugitives in an almost legalistic form. They begin to create a

David E.E. Sloane, "Huck Acts, an Escape from Civilization," in *Adventures of Huckleberry Finn, American Comic Vision*, Boston, MA: Twayne, 1988, pp. 50–60. Copyright © 1988 by G.K. Hall & Co. All rights reserved. Reproduced by permission of Gale, a part of Cengage Learning.

world and an ethic which will distinguish their raft on the Mississippi as one of the great American images of freedom and brotherhood. Tom Sawyer had also gone to Jackson's Island, in fact, and left the people on shore as sure of his death as they now are of Huck's. In the sentence-by-sentence texture of Huck's observations and objectives, however, tremendous differences can be discovered between his persona and Tom's.

Leaving Society Behind

As the reader is initiated into the raft journey, he is also almost immediately initiated into Huck and Jim's more caring relationship, and sees Huck as a deeper mentality than Tom with simpler and more immediate concerns of food, safety, and survival. Because of Huck's dry humor and because of the more compelling results of his actions in regard to Jim, Huck is both detached from others and involved with them. His detachment is far more adult and Twainian than was Tom Sawyer's. Huck's closeness in mutual simplicity and sympathy with Jim provides him with his personal basis for abandoning the restrictions of the authorities of the village, their laws, and their public opinion.

Jackson's Island is first seen in the night, "big and dark and solid, like a steamboat without any lights." A big lumber raft is also seen coming, and Huck hears the voices of the men, one of Twain's many suggestions of heightened powers of perception on the river. After Huck naps, he wakes "in the grass and cool shade, thinking about things and feeling rested and rather comfortable": this is only the second time in the novel that he has registered "comfort." With "friendly" squirrels overhead, and feeling "powerful lazy and comfortable," Huck has attained the real boy's ideal state as identified in the literature of the realistic bad boys of the post–Civil War era. . . .

A Partnership

Setting up housekeeping on the island, Huck occupies himself first with a businesslike examination of his island. Becoming "boss" of the island in a rather professional way, discovering both snakes, which will soon figure in the action, and the still-smoking ashes of a campfire, he is driven up a tree, out in a canoe, and finally into stealthy woodcraft and sophisticated detective work. Jim and Huck are quickly united at this point, for the ashes turn out to be Jim's fire, at which he is discovered sleeping the next night. Huck is, once again, taken for a dead person. But finally recognized as a live one, he enters into partnership with Jim. Huck and Jim establish at once the motif of mutual trust. Huck feels certain that he can count on *him* (Twain putting the pronoun for Jim in italics) not to tell. The sense of security in flight first goes Huck's way in this novel, since both Huck and Jim came to the island three days previously, shortly after Huck was killed, as Twain has Huck say it, using their easy literality to create verbal humor. They share a meal and comfort before Jim offers his confidence, in turn, to Huck.

Jim almost immediately, but with some caution, relies on Huck as deeply as Huck has relied on him. When Jim says that he *run off* (Twain again using italics, now for Jim's secret), it is couched amidst promises extracted from Huck not to tell. Huck even adds the proper ambivalence to his not telling by saying that people would call him a "low down Ablitionist and despise me," but he isn't going back there anyway—an early but clear statement that leaving a social setting frees the frontiersman from its flawed social beliefs and hatred of nonconformists. Yet Huck has been shown to have at first blush the continuing conscience of his community—as expressed earlier in Miss Watson's holding slaves and Pap's attitude toward "free niggers." For Huck and Jim, reciprocity is established in this initial interchange. Both are involved in life and death flights. Huck's defining battle later will be to retain his focus directly on the personalized ethic—his heart—which overcomes abstract ideas such as those which govern his antagonists.

Heart and Nature

Jackson's Island is still a place of nature as it was in *Adventures of Tom Sawyer*, but its quality is now joined to the problem of Huck's survival, Jim's freedom, and social ostracism. Tom observed an inchworm and went on playing; when Jim observes the birds flying low and predicts rain, he and Huck superstitiously move to higher ground, are saved from the rising river, and end up enjoying hot cornbread in their cave, secure above the flood. Huck's description of the thunderstorm includes metaphors of hell in references to "dark as sin" and "the underside of the world." For Huck and Jim, their folk superstition has saved them where religiosity would have been useless. This position contrary to Miss Watson's is developed through Twain's use of natural images and occurrences. . . .

The ongoing considerations of how good is achieved, whether through religious or personal acts, is reviewed in caricature. These events lead Jim to reflect on slavery and the expropriation of a human being's value: "I owns myself, en I's wuth eight hund'd dollars. I wisht I had de money, I wouldn't want no mo." Jim's reference to his value as a slave foreshadows his urge to buy his wife and children out of slavery. Thus, even silliness on Jackson's Island leads inevitably back into Huck and Jim's personalities, their safety, and the crucial social issues surrounding their lives. Snakes and practical jokes add further dimensions. The island *would* have to be "big and solid" to support this heavy a freight of the novel's developing themes. . . .

A Change in Attitude

Huck's forgetfulness of natural rules causes him to nearly kill Jim when he attempts to play his first joke on Jim by curling a snakeskin in Jim's blankets. Huck's "ever so natural" joke is almost deadly as the snake's mate strikes Jim. The snake skin is a Tom Sawyer practical joke, but is significantly milder than the later stories of Bricksville loafers who like to set stray dogs on fire or tie tin pans to their tails to see them run themselves to death. In part, harsh-seeming practical jokes are part of Twain's realism, for country-style practical jokes are sometimes cruel beyond what contemporary urban-dwellers could imagine; earlier regional humorists—not only those of the Southwest—recorded many in their writings. However, hiding a snakeskin in Jim's blankets to frighten him is also, at the literary level, an example of the pattern of Tom going from play and more personal action to "effects" on other people, such as his aunt or the schoolmaster. When Huck attempts the same pattern, Jim is reduced to pulling on Pap's jug and declines into near-convulsions and death. His recovery takes four days and nights. Notably, Jim gets out of his head like Pap, and Pap is named and included in the resultant events, thus recalling as a consequence the novel's ugliest and most degraded scene. Since this action was Huck's, "all my fault," his embarrassment is an appropriate outcome—one which Twain will build on as Huck and Jim progress on the raft after the storm. After this first practical joke, Huck will make one more before abandoning such effects. Reasonably enough, the joke episodes are taken by most critics as crucial stages in Huck's maturation, and their use to show Huck's changing respect for Jim is clear evidence of how events are packed in the narrative, giving it a far more dramatic emotional development than occurs in *Tom Sawyer*. . . .

"They're After Us!"

Huck, of course, has his own set of hidden allegiances, developed in the previous episodes, to Jim, and so uses all his skills to secure Jim's escape, carefully noting times, doubling back, and lighting a decoy campfire to throw off pursuit. Huck quickly arouses Jim: "Git up and hump yourself, Jim! There-ain't a minute to lose. They're after us!" This use of the word "us" represents the full joining of the fates of the two refugees: "Jim never asked no questions, he never said a word; but the way he worked for the next half an hour showed about how he was scared. By that time everything we had in the world was on our raft. . . ." Without lights, "dead still, without saying a word," Huck and Jim on the raft slip below the tip of Jackson's Island—and—in silence and darkness, without any fanfare of false "style"—begin the greatest literary voyage in later nineteenth-century fiction.

Huck's Tricks and Jim's Deception

Forrest G. Robinson

Forrest G. Robinson, professor of American studies at the University of California–Santa Cruz, is the author of The New Western History: The Territory Ahead and The Author-Cat: Clemens's Life in Fiction.

In the following piece, Forrest G. Robinson brings a new dimension to the character of Jim: his desperation to stay alive after he runs away, his dependence on Huck as his only hope, and his taking on of a submissive role in the last chapters at the Phelps farm to have at least a chance to save his own life. But the idealism with which we tend to read the Huck/Jim friendship is not the whole story. The frequent and often mean tricks Huck plays on Jim reveal his ambivalence toward a black man. Jim also injects a degree of realism and self-interest into their relationship by withholding knowledge of Pap's death from Huck and, after the idyllic trip down the Mississippi, taking on the mask of silent submission.

The London *Saturday Review* for 31 January 1885 carried a review of *Huckleberry Finn* by Brander Matthews, an American who would in later years become a professor at Columbia University. In the midst of much that is apt and insightful, Matthews observes that Jim, the escaped slave who accompanies Huck downriver on the raft, displays "the essential simplicity and kindliness and generosity of the Southern negro." This general impression of Jim has been challenged only very rarely in the century since the novel first appeared.

Forrest G. Robinson, "The Characterization of Jim in *Huckleberry Finn*," *Nineteenth Century Literature*, vol. 33, no. 3, December 1988, pp. 361–391. Copyright © 1988 by The Regents of the University of California. Reproduced by permission of the publisher and the author.

But in place of Matthews's obvious approval of Mark Twain's treatment of Jim, more recent critics have been strongly inclined to contrast the submissive slave who appears in the closing chapters with the more complete human being who moves through the central sections of the narrative. Modern observers are in broad agreement that this simpler, more passive Jim is radically out of character. He is a mere fragment of his former self, a two-dimensional parody, a racial stereotype with roots in the minstrel tradition, and one symptom among many others of Mark Twain's failure of moral vision and artistic integrity in the complex evasion that closes the action. . . .

The Necessity to Assume a Role

It is not my intention to take issue with the view that the submissive, all-suffering Jim of the concluding "evasion" chapters contrasts rather sharply with the forthright, assertive, essentially good but fully rounded human being who appears in the central sections of the novel. Jim does seem to change, from a plausibly complete man to an apparently incomplete, two-dimensional racial stereotype. At the same time, however, I want to raise the possibility that this major transformation in Jim's appearance can be brought into clear alignment with a coherent analysis of his characterization. Jim changes, I want to argue, because he sees that he must. I find that Jim's characterization is profoundly true to the realities of his experience in the novel; but it is culturally true as well in the apparent inconsistency that it has seemed, in the eyes of the audience, to betray. In this latter, cultural framework, it is not Jim's character that finally requires explanation; rather, it is the general failure to recognize the necessity and significance of his retreat to passivity that we must attend to. . . .

Jim's circumstances could hardly be more perilous. He is a runaway slave in the territory; and he is a leading suspect in what is perceived to be Huck's murder. For white people who know him, he is the object of angry pursuit; for those who do not—as subsequent episodes demonstrate—he is an object of suspicion and heartless grasping after quick profits.

So bereft, Jim must run by night, hide by day, and through it all endure loneliness, fear verging toward panic, and a crippling lack of information. He reveals his sense of his predicament best when he reports to Huck how it felt to be stranded on the *Walter Scott*.

> He said that when I went in the texas and he crawled back to get on the raft and found her gone, he nearly died; because he judged it was all up with *him*, anyway it could be fixed; for if he didn't get saved he would get drownded; and if he did get saved, whoever saved him would send him back home so as to get the reward, and then Miss Watson would sell him south, sure.

Saved or not saved, Jim feels doom closing down on him. Little wonder, then, that he is always gratified to see Huck. Jim may in time come to love the white boy; but from the beginning he needs him desperately. Huck is the living proof that Jim is not a murderer. And Huck gives him eyes and ears, information, an alibi, and some small leverage when the inevitable disaster strikes. On those subsequent occasions when Jim welcomes Huck back to the raft, this desperate need, and the sense of breathless relief, provide the warmth in what usually passes for unmingled outbursts of affection. The boy is Jim's best chance for survival; naturally, he is pleased to have him back.

Huck's is one of very few faces that Jim can be happy to see. But in order to get a proper hold on the deep mutuality of the relationship between the man and child, we must recognize that the generalization works equally well in reverse. When Huck discovers that his companion on Jackson's Island is Miss Watson's Jim, his enthusiasm is immediately manifest: "I bet I was glad to see him," he reflects. Huck's remarks are often taken to express his respect and friendship for Jim.

There may be some of this in his attitude, but in larger part his pleasure has its foundation in relief—and unlooked for relief at that. Upon first discovering Jim's camp, Huck recoils in fear. He is afraid that he will be recognized, and that his desperate scheme to get away from his father will be revealed, leaving him more perilously vulnerable than ever to Pap's really pathological violence. . . .

Huck's Tricks

Huck's impulse to play mean tricks on Jim, and his decision to turn him over to the authorities, arise out of an ambivalence about Jim, and about black people generally, that is in turn rooted in the racist ideology of white society. Huck is free enough of the dominant culture to respond to Jim as a human being; but he is also prone to sudden reversals of feeling that betray his deep immersion in the mentality of the white majority. This dividedness in Huck is conspicuously at work in his cruel joke with the "trash" (after he and Jim have been separated in the fog), his prompt apology, his equally sudden decision to betray Jim, and the brilliant, spontaneous deception of the predatory slave hunters that immediately follows. These abrupt, radical reversals are evidence of the boy's wavering marginality, and speak clearly to his restlessness in the ambiguous ties that bind him to Jim. . . .

Jim's Deception

While we may wince at Huck's racist condescension, we should also reflect on the clear suggestion that Jim nourishes this attitude in order that he may exploit the blindness that accompanies it. Jim's maneuvering bears the further suggestion that he is from the very outset uneasy with Huck, alert to his acquiescence in the ideology of the slave system, and aware that the boy's best intentions are only half of a perilously divided sensibility. It is hardly surprising that Jim should feel this way; events certainly bear him out. Indeed, it would be surprising if

Eddie Hodges as Huck and Archie Moore as Jim in the 1960 film adaptation of Huckleberry Finn. *After their separation on the river, Jim rejoins Huck on the raft but is more cautious and less forthcoming.* Grey Villet/Time Life Pictures/Getty Images.

he did not observe all due caution in his dealings with the boy whose good-heartedness does nothing to conceal his acculturation to white ways of thinking. When Jim reluctantly admits the truth to Huck—"I—I *run off*"—he cannot fail to perceive the shock of disapproval in Huck's response: "Jim!". And that is why he is so cautious with Huck, so careful to confirm the boy's prejudiced expectations before moving carefully, imperceptibly beyond them. . . .

Turning the Stereotype to Advantage

Working against this larger cultural background, it remains to complete the analysis of Jim's maneuvering for survival, as we may glimpse it, most often obliquely, within the web of deception and concealment that the culture—and the narrative—casts around him. Most crucially, we have determined that he is neither as gullible nor as passive nor as stupidly good-natured as the stereotype of the slave would have him. On the contrary, it is one measure of his estimable resourcefulness that he contrives to turn this stereotype to his own advantage. He maneuvers behind the mask that the white oppressors, in bad faith denial of their fear and guilt, have thrust upon him. He is, we have seen, a master of self-interested simulation and dissimulation, though it is clear as well—most especially in his ultimate disclosure about Pap—that he is not deceived by his own acts of deception. We may now advance a step further in this line of analysis, to observe that while Jim is not the fool of his own acts of deception, he is not blind to the fact that other people—most often white people—are. . . .

Jim's Silence and Wariness

The reunion of the fugitives after the feud section in chapters 17–18 is clear evidence that Jim feels more secure with Huck's company on the raft than he does without it. Huck may be trouble, but he is also intermittently a vital resource. At the same time, Jim is chastened and cautious in rejoining Huck, and displays a resolve to retreat behind a mask of silence and unquestioning compliance. We see and hear much less of Jim, in the remainder of the novel. To an extent, of course, this is because the action turns away from him; but he is also quite markedly inclined to turn away from the action when it comes his way. Jim has tried being "visible" and frank, opinionated, assertive, even argumentative with Huck, and the invariable result has been trouble. He has come to see that Huck, for all of his good nature, is quite unprepared to tolerate the full unfolding of the human being emergent from behind the mask of the happy, gullible, rather childlike slave. At no little price in suffering and danger, Jim finally learns to apply to Huck the formula that he earlier advocated for relations with all mean and quarrelsome white people: "if we minded our business and didn't talk back and aggravate them, we would pull through." . . .

Seeing a Complete Jim

We return again and again to *Huckleberry Finn* not only because it permits us to ignore as much of the truth about race-slavery as we cannot bear to see, but also because in enabling our bad faith denial—a brand of denial clearly cognate with those dramatized in the novel itself—*Huckleberry Finn* leaves us with the uneasy feeling that we have missed something, and thereby ensures that we will return for another look. One such perpetual oversight—and surely a kind of key to all the others—is the character Jim I have labored to reach in this essay. But the image of the happy, gullible, superstitious "darky" can never be fully separated from its background in injustice and cruelty and suffering, and from the pressure of resistance behind the bland, smiling face. That separation cannot occur in spite of the fact—and perhaps finally because of the fact— that such a separation is the urgent cultural objective toward which the formation and wide reception of that image move. The stereotype that informs Jim was conceived in the unconscious wish that it might draw attention away from the disagreeable tendency of its human model to suffer pain and to resent it; but the trace of that submerged dimension is present, at the very least by conspicuous absence, in the bland, selfless, almost mindless figure who appears at intervals toward the end of Mark Twain's novel. Prima facie ["at first view"] the stereotype is incomplete. If we are willing to press against our first impressions of the text, we find that a fuller, much more plausible human figure is present by nearly palpable implication in the two-dimensional mask. But the character also gives us more than we are initially prepared to see; and if we are willing to move further in this direction, we find that the two-dimensional figure has roots, submerged but within reach of recovery, in the bad faith cultural dynamics of our own response. Thus by becoming more attentive to the curve of Jim's development, from a kind of tentative candor and completeness to virtual submergence in the minstrel figure, we are well positioned to learn something about the complex dynamics of his apparent transformation, and about the cultural construction of the role he retreats to.

Counter Conversion

Norris W. Yates

Norris W. Yates is Mellon Professor of English at the University of Pittsburgh. He has written on a variety of topics and published Gender and Genre *and* Gunter Grass.

Norris W. Yates argues in the following essay that religion plays a significant part in Huck Finn's decisions regarding Jim, having been indoctrinated by Miss Watson, a superreligious slave owner. Huck comes out of a religious society that supports slavery, sees slaves as subhuman, and abolitionists as thieves. Thus, in this society, helping Jim escape is the worst form of wickedness. But Huck's crises of conscience, while they have religious frames, turn out to be the opposite of traditional conversion. He appears at first to be considering conversion to religious goodness when he writes a letter telling Miss Watson of Jim's whereabouts. But immediately he tears it up and decides to "go to hell," giving up his immortal soul to save a black man.

One of the major thematic strands in *Huckleberry Finn* is Huck's struggle with his conscience and his decision "to go to hell" rather than to assist in returning Jim to servitude. The part played by these events in Mark Twain's castigation of a society both pious and proslavery has been emphasized in a general way. Yet the manner in which Huck's inner conflict dramatizes the specifically religious elements in that society has been little more than mentioned. . . . Few students of the novel have said . . . much about the part religion plays in Huck's struggle and decision.

Norris W. Yates, "The Counter Conversion of Huckleberry Finn," *American Literature*, vol. 32, no. 1, March 1, 1960, pp. 1–10. Copyright © 1960 by the Duke University Press. All rights reserved. Copyright renewed 1988 by the Duke University Press. Used by permission of the publisher.

Conversion in Reverse

An intensive study of Huck's moments of moral crisis concerning Jim leads one to see that Huck, whatever else he may be, is in a number of important particulars a sinner struggling for conversion; it leads further to the suggestion that he is indeed "converted"—in reverse; he undergoes a "counter-conversion" to "wickedness" which is in part an ironic consequence of his religious training. . . .

A person may be converted many times, and Huck is converted, or counter-converted, twice. In Chapter XVI he decides to tell two white men that Jim is a runaway slave. In Chapter XXXI he writes a letter to Miss Watson which will inform her that Jim is being held by Mr. Phelps. However, he declares his willingness to go to hell and tears the letter up. In this willingness lies his permanent "conversion" into "unregeneracy."

Huck's changes of moral attitude are foreshadowed in several earlier passages. In the first chapter he is attracted by Miss Watson's description of "the bad place," but her account of heaven, "the good place," leaves him cold. In Chapter III Huck decides that there are "two Providences" and that he prefers the widow's, but as he sees the matter, Providence in any form is that of a slaveholding society and heaven belongs to the respectable. Because Huck is not respectable he finds it easy to believe later on that he is shut out from heaven. Foreshadowing of the ironic sort occurs in Chapter V when Pap Finn, having scolded Huck for going to school, says, "First you know you'll get religion too." Of course Huck already has "got religion" in the sense that he is a believer in heaven and hell, and he never ceases to believe in them or in slavery as an institution. But Huck's ultimate decision to turn against the Fugitive Slave Law would have been an offense to Pap Finn as well as to the proslavery churchgoers of the Mississippi valley.

"They're After Us"

On Jackson's Island Huck rouses Jim with the news that a search party is on the way. "They're after us!" is his cry. [Critic]

Leo Marx has stressed the inadvertent use of "us." Even this early in their relationship Huck has unconsciously formed the habit of identifying himself with Jim and is thus already beginning to think of him as a person rather than as a chattel [piece of property]. This habit is strengthened on the raft. . . . For some time Huck remains unaware of this step-by-step growth of a new attitude within the shell of the conscious view imposed by piety and property. The new attitude makes a thrust into partial consciousness when Huck forces himself to apologize to Jim for having tricked him into believing that their separation in the fog was only a dream. His apology itself is an act of will but he is unconscious that any deeper change is involved than that of merely doing Jim "no more mean tricks." However, unconscious habit-formation is making Huck ready for a more reflective decision. . . .

The Religious Element

Huck's second and final bout of soul-searching over Jim is in part a repetition of the first; the chief difference is the addition of a religious element that is partly overt and partly unconscious. Since his first conversion Huck has read "considerable" in *Pilgrim's Progress*, which he found "interesting but tough," and he has listened to a sermon about brotherly love preached to the Grangerfords and Shepherdsons as they sat in church with their guns handy. From some of these same guntoters he has heard conversation about "faith, and good works, and free grace, and preforeordestination," and he feels that this was "one of the roughest Sundays I had run across yet." . . .

This second crisis is precipitated by the king's having turned Jim in to white law; the enormity of the deed (which the duke has abetted) shocks Huck into sustained reflection. Jim is being held at the Phelpses and Huck at first thinks of making this disclosure to Miss Watson through Tom Sawyer but rejects the idea partly because of his natural sympathy for

Jim and partly because he is still afraid to lose what little is left of his respectability by helping "a nigger to get his freedom." . . .

Like many converts, Huck knows that he is "playing double" and holding on to sin. Having found out at last that he cannot "pray a lie," he is "full of trouble" and tries to gain peace by writing to Miss Watson that Jim has been caught. Once he has actually written the letter, he expresses his feeling of release in one of the more common pulpit metaphors: "I felt good and all washed clean of sin for the first time I had ever felt so in my life, and I knowed I could pray now." Here is a possible echo from the camp meeting, where Huck had heard one of the preachers shout "'the waters that cleanse is free.'" Here also is a figure used by other converts to describe their state of mind at the moment of the great change.

But here, as in his first moral crisis, Huck's apparent conversion is only the prelude to a counter-conversion. Although he offers no explanation of why, having written the letter, he does not pray immediately, the reason is plain: his feeling for Jim is at the point of bursting into full consciousness. . . .

Religious Approval of Slavery

But in assisting Jim, Huck is torn by the contradiction in a religious way of life that approves of both altruism and slavery, although he cannot put it to himself in those terms. The result is a minor triumph of irony: first Huck tries to pray for strength to help send Jim back to Miss Watson; one of his purposes is thus to do that lady a service. The widow could not logically have disapproved of his version of why he cannot pray a lie; such "playing double" as Huck does is not agreeable to the Lord's will and he knows it, and this knowledge contributes to his abandonment of any further effort at salvation. The widow would doubtless have considered Huck's altruistic wish to help Jim at the risk of hellfire a bit extreme, but her own advice has played a part in the development of that wish.

Hell

Another aspect of Huck's training to which his wrong-way regeneration owes something is the . . . conception of eternal punishment. Huck knows that there can be no degrees of condemnation; he therefore expects to suffer the maximum penalty. Since he has nothing more to lose, he resolves to help Jim again. Actually he has been aiding and abetting Jim's bid for freedom from the moment he first encountered the runaway on Jackson's Island. But the authoritative view of damnation aids him in the "unification of character" in which his consciously willed desire becomes the same as his previous instinctive one. Thus Huck's absorbing of three major elements in frontier fundamentalism—its endorsement of slavery, its views on prayer, and its version of hell—have been applied in an ironically reverse fashion to bring about his counter-conversion into official reprobation and actual goodness.

No two conversion cases are exactly alike, and Huck's conversion is lacking in several elements found in many. He shows no special desire to love God or to achieve union with Him. Christ is not even mentioned; Satan too as an anthropomorphic force is absent from his reflections. Nevertheless Huck's experience in reaching his decision may be viewed either as an incomplete conversion followed by backsliding or as a counter-conversion which turns out to be permanent. By presenting part of Huck's moral growth within the pattern of a religious phenomenon that was widespread in rural America, and in a sense, by turning that pattern upside-down, Mark Twain supplied ingredients in the irony of the novel which deserve closer attention.

Losing Brotherhood in the "Evasion"

Arthur G. Pettit

Arthur G. Pettit is the author of Mark Twain and the South *and the editor of* Images of the Mexican American in Fiction and Film.

In this article, Arthur G. Pettit argues that while Jim is "the conscience" of the novel, his humanizing influence seems to evaporate once he and Huck leave the river. Although as a white boy, Huck can provide protection for Jim, it is really Jim's superior experience and intelligence that guide Huck. And it is Jim's superior affection that fosters Huck's moral sense. On the river, with his confessions of his own weakness, Jim is humanized in Huck's eyes. With the evasion section, the humanity of Jim disappears into stereotype as Tom Sawyer enters the scene and Huck submits to Tom's cruel fantasies. In light of this reversal, that smacks of Mark Twain's cynicism about the possibility of racial harmony, what stays with readers is the impossible dream of the river's freedom and brotherhood.

Nigger Jim is the conscience of *Huckleberry Finn*. More than Huck he is the moral standard by which other characters in the novel are measured and found wanting. This black man is a new kind of character in American fiction, a highly complex and original creation.

Jim's Influence on Huck

Huck learns compassion from Jim. Without this black man the boy's rebelliousness would be confined to petty stealing, lying, putting his feet up on the widow's furniture, and run-

Arthur G. Pettit, "Everything All Busted Up and Ruined: The Fate of Brotherhood," in *Mark Twain and the South*, New York: The University Press of Kentucky, 1974, pp. 109–122. Previously unpublished material from the Mark Twain Papers at the University of California at Berkeley, copyright © 1973 by the trustees under the will of Clara Clemens Samossoud. Used by permission of the trustees of the Mark Twain Estate.

ning away. Jim makes Huck's revolt more than a personal re-action to etiquette and niceties; when Jim is taken from the raft and put in prison, Huck loses the stature he gained from being with a black man. It is this feeling of heart and expression of conscience, exhibited by a black and emulated by a white, that makes the relationship between Nigger Jim and Huck memorable. It is the central theme of *Huckleberry Finn* and the most appealing dream of interracial brotherhood in our literature.

Huck and Jim first meet in the novel on the level they will assume whenever superstition is at issue; Jim as teacher, Huck as learner. When the boy sees his father's tracks in the snow, he sets out at once to discover how it is that Pap, whom he has not seen for a year and had hoped was dead, is after all alive and about. To find out what Pap is up to, Huck goes to the highest possible authority—Nigger Jim's hairball oracle.

At this point the two future companions are casual acquaintances, brought together because they are both in the power of white women. . . .

When Pap gets drunk and almost kills him, Huck simulates his own murder and flees to Jackson's Island. There he meets Jim. Both are fugitives fleeing from their respective forms of bondage—Jim from Miss Watson whose Christian principles could not withstand a slave trader's offer of eight hundred dollars, Huck from the disagreeable alternatives of Miss Watson's peckings and Pap's beatings.

Jim's Knowledge and Affection

Huck pretends to be Jim's protector, but Jim is the one who actually lays the groundwork for a satisfactory relationship. His readings of the signs of nature are accurate and his folk cures usually work. It is Jim who suggests that they seek higher ground in the cave before the arrival of the storm which would have drowned them, Jim who builds the wigwam on the raft captured in the June flood, Jim who finds Pap's body in the floating house of death and shields Huck from the knowledge by covering Pap's face. . . .

He is also Huck's superior in affection and loyalty. Knowing that Pap is dead, and denied the opportunity to lavish affection on his own family, Jim takes on the role of foster father to an orphan boy. He calls Huck "honey," "boss," and other pet names and vows, to Huck, that he will never "forgit you . . . honey." Huck on the other hand is in no shape at the outset to enter into a relationship that requires equal respect or affection. Even though he despises tricks and jokes of all kinds, he tricks Jim several times. . . .

Huck's Growing Humanity

Huck hesitates to abandon this ideal way station between civilization and savagery. He does so only when he thinks he has to: learning from Mrs. Loftus that slave hunters are approaching the island looking for Jim, Huck forgets that no one is after *him* (he is, after all, officially dead), and shouts the three words—"They're after us!"—that constitute his first real commitment to Jim. When the two fugitives push the raft out into the dark and flooded river, Huck, though he is not yet willing to admit it, has finally become a "low-down Abolitionist."

Once on the river the boy begins to show some real affection for Jim, in part because he is bound to the black man by nighttime travel on the raft, in part because he is getting lonely. The words lonesome, loneliness, and lonely occur repeatedly on the river, rarely while Huck is on shore. Indeed the river provides an opportunity for a measure of compassion and commitment that Huck never would have tolerated on Jackson's Island. Before going ashore to try to save the thieves stranded on the sinking *Walter Scott*, he carefully hides Jim. Later, on one of the few occasions when the two find themselves on the river in daylight, Huck makes Jim lie down in the canoe "because if he set up people could tell he was a nigger a good ways off."

The change in Huck is especially striking when he begins automatically to share with Jim. He divides the loot taken from the *Walter Scott* and splits the forty dollars that the two slave hunters float over the water to save his family from the smallpox. . . .

Complexity of Morality

The moral distance between Huck's disregard for Jim's feelings for the child in the Solomon episode and the boy's compassion for Jim's confession of his own abuse of his deaf and dumb daughter suggests how far the two have traveled together. The surest indication that this black man has finally been accepted as human is Huck's willingness to accept his fallibility. It is Jim's capacity for both cruelty and remorse that places him solidly within the wicked and contrite human race. The insensitivity, violence, and remorseful suffering attributed by the author to his character is also the best indication of Mark Twain's great if erratic capacity for accepting a black man as a man.

Two moral lessons, the Solomon story and Jim's confession about his daughter, prepare the way for Huck's three great moral crises in the novel. The first occurs when he springs still another joke on Jim, but this time accepts the consequences and humbles himself to a black man. The second occurs when Huck almost betrays Jim to the slave hunters on the river. The third, and the high point of the book, comes when Huck wrestles with his conscience, whips it, and decides to free Jim from reenslavement and to be damned. Each is a different kind of study in the boy's growing commitment to Jim. . . .

Battling Religion

Repeatedly in his final agony Huck must do battle with the theological jargon he has picked up from Southern sermons upholding slavery. We recall that earlier in the novel Miss

Scene from the 1960 movie adaptation of Huckleberry Finn *with Archie Moore as Jim and Eddie Hodges as Huck. On the Mississippi River, Jim becomes Huck's moral teacher.* Grey Villet/Time Life Pictures/Getty Images.

Watson prattled on about heaven and good works, while plotting to sell Jim down the river. Now Huck, her unregenerate pupil, thinks "awful thoughts" and says "awful things" that would have shocked Miss Watson, all the while plotting somehow to keep in God's graces *and* free Jim. Realizing finally that he can't have it both ways, Huck sits down at the edge of the river which gave him his largest measure of freedom and, to avoid damnation, beseeches God's help in turning Jim in, but "the words wouldn't come." Failing in prayer, he writes the letter to Miss Watson to save his soul. . . .

Huck tears up the letter and risks hell. Though he frets most over the crippled clichés of Southern Calvinism, we are likely to be more impressed with the careful manner in which he separates Jim from slavery. Huck's decision to free Jim is not prompted by moral insight or outrage, but by the memory of Jim on the river. Slavery hasn't been dislodged; it is only Jim who is no longer for sale. Huck will be damned for devotion to a single black man, not for repudiation of the peculiar institution *as* an institution. In the most ingenious irony in the novel an immoral, poor white boy behaves like a Christian by rejecting Christianity, does right by doing wrong, and, in doing so, widens the gap between himself and the respectable, religious, and righteous South.

Controversial Evasion

But then there is the end of the novel, an ending that comprises one-quarter of the book. For many readers the notorious evasion episode on the Phelps's farm is a peculiarly well-named disaster—a device for quite literally evading the complex moral issues Mark Twain had raised on the river.

Critics agree that the problem lies in the reappearance of Tom Sawyer, who in defiance of the laws of fictional probability turns out to be related to the family holding Jim in bondage, Uncle Silas and Aunt Sally Phelps. When Tom comes down from St. Petersburg to Pikesville, Arkansas, for a visit, he already knows that Jim is a free man, freed by Miss Watson herself. But he tells no one and at once takes the lead in liberating Jim. . . .

We expect this kind of behavior from Tom. Far more upsetting is the fact that Huck, after discovering on a thousand miles of river the folly of tormenting a black man, contributes some indelicacies of his own. He worries that Jim may not survive the number of years it will take to surround his prison with moats and to dig him out through solid rock with kitchen knives. . . .

If Huck suffers a serious decline, Jim is reduced to the level of farce. When Tom and Huck enter his prison on the Phelps's farm, he cries for the fourth time in the novel and makes it clear that he is eager to be gone. But the white boys prevail upon him ("Jim he said it was all right") to endure three weeks of vaudeville stunts that approach sadism and leave them all "pretty much fagged out . . . but mainly Jim." . . .

The evasion episode leads to two disturbing conclusions about the relationship between Jim and Huck and the fate of interracial brotherhood in *Huckleberry Finn*. Mark Twain's constant shuffling between sympathy, pathos, disinterest, and even hostility toward Jim suggests that he could not make up his mind about where this black man stood in his scheme for the novel. In a state of nature Jim is noble. On shore he is a comic buffoon. . . .

The End of Jim's Role

In a nineteenth-century book about a slave society as seen through the eyes of a white boy, Jim can be the conscience of the novel but he cannot be the main character. By the end of chapter 31 Jim's function as moral instructor is over, with one-quarter of the action ahead. Indeed one could say that Jim assumed the role of Huck's moral instructor on the river only at the risk of becoming the boy's moral burden on the shore—and one that eventually became too great for Huck. After deciding to free Jim the boy willingly, even gratefully, turned the task over to Tom Sawyer. The implications of such a desertion are awesome and portentous: blacks may for a time act as the white man's conscience, but sooner or later that conscience becomes too much to bear. Such subtleties of course are lost on Jim as well as on Huck. At the end of the novel, clutching his forty-dollar gift "for being prisoner for us so patient," the liberated black man is "pleased most to death" with the way things have turned out. "*Dah*, now, Huck," he boasts, "what I tell you? . . . I *tole* you I got a hairy breas', en . . . gwineter to be rich . . . en heah she *is!*" The moments on the river have been forgotten.

Twain's Pessimism

The second conclusion about Jim and Huck goes beyond the novel to take in Mark Twain's growing pessimism about the possibility for any sort of permanent interracial harmony or brotherhood. . . . While on the raft, Huck and Jim try to practice a code of compassion and decency. "What you want, above all things, on a raft," Huck explains, "is for everybody to be satisfied, and feel right and kind towards the others." But their intentions are constantly thwarted by nature and by men. . . .

The most excruciating irony of all is that the flight down the river has nothing whatever to do with Jim's final attainment of freedom. Poor Miss Watson, whose greed started the two down the Mississippi in the first place, provides that. Though this woman's deathbed manumission [emancipation] is plausible, when Jim gains his freedom through the last will and testament of one of the novel's most unlikable characters we . . . feel cheated: Jim's liberation on land will probably bring him less freedom than he enjoyed as a slave on the river, and it certainly spells the end of a possible relationship of equality with Huck. Jim can be freed from bondage but not from the disability of being black. To acknowledge this is to admit that the final fate of brotherhood in *Huckleberry Finn* is as disappointing as it is realistic. If freedom and brotherhood are possible only outside of society—if blacks and whites can really know each other only in isolation from other men— then there is not going to be very much brotherhood. Love and nature are not enough. With this admission, one of the high hopes of *Huckleberry Finn* goes down to defeat, drowned at the river's edge. As Huck says after the King sells Jim, the journey really *has* come to nothing. Everything, indeed, is "all busted up and ruined."

An Enduring, Impossible Dream

However, to end here would be another form of cheating. There *is* another dimension to the novel that transcends defeat. If the end of *Huckleberry Finn* suggests the way things are, the river portion of the novel provokes our sense of the way things ought to be. . . .

• What the raft and the river come to mean is a marvelous condition of unreality—a shucking of our bondage to men, time, and codes of morality in exchange for a kind of freedom and companionship that can never be reached on shore. Long after Tom Sawyer's evasion has blurred into the background of our memory, the image of a black man and a white boy on a raft remains—a fantasy of brotherhood as appealing as it was perishable.

In Defense of *Adventures of Huckleberry Finn*

Toni Morrison

Toni Morrison is Robert F. Goheen Professor Emerita on the Council of the Humanities at Princeton University and an internationally recognized novelist who won the Pulitzer Prize in 1988 and the Nobel Prize in 1993.

In the following excerpt, consisting of about half of the original introduction, Toni Morrison expresses her own unease after multiple encounters with Twain's novel, beginning with independent childhood readings, followed by a reading in junior high school, and several readings as an adult. She came to see that Huck's internalized misery and fear were somehow assuaged by the presence of Jim. Even though the story closes with Jim as a minstrel figure, there are "undertows," she contends, one of which is the similarity between the ante- and postbellum South. The black man becomes the white boy's surrogate father—his "father for free"—as Morrison puts it. The three problems that the novel ends with are Huck Finn's outcast situation even at the end; the sadness in his and Jim's relationship; and Huck's engagement with racism during the evasion. The question remains: will Huck actually escape the evils of civilization by going West?

Fear and alarm are what I remember most about my first encounter with Mark Twain's *Adventures of Huckleberry Finn*. Palpable alarm. . . . My second reading of it, under the supervision of an English teacher in junior high school, was no less uncomfortable—rather more. It provoked a feeling I can only describe now as muffled rage, as though appreciation of the work required my complicity in and sanction of something shaming. . . .

In the early eighties I read *Huckleberry Finn* again, provoked, I believe, by demands to remove the novel from the libraries and required reading lists of public schools. These efforts were based, it seemed to me, on a narrow notion of how to handle the offense Mark Twain's use of the term "nigger" would occasion for black students and the corrosive effect it would have on white ones. It struck me as a purist yet elementary kind of censorship designed to appease adults rather than educate children. Amputate the problem, band-aid the solution. A serious comprehensive discussion of the term by an intelligent teacher certainly would have benefited my eighth-grade class and would have spared all of us (a few blacks, many whites—mostly second-generation immigrant children) some grief. . . .

Although its language—sardonic, photographic, persuasively aural—and the structural use of the river as control and chaos seem to me quite the major feats of *Huckleberry Finn*, much of the novel's genius lies in its quiescence, the silences that pervade it and give it a porous quality that is by turns brooding and soothing. . . . A plaintive note of melancholy and dread surfaces immediately in the first chapter, after Huck sums up the narrative of his life in a prior book. . . .

Although Huck complains bitterly of rules and regulations, I see him to be running not from external control but from external chaos. Nothing in society makes sense; all is in peril. Upper-class, churchgoing, elegantly housed families annihilate themselves in a psychotic feud, and Huck has to drag two of their corpses from the water—one of whom is a just-made friend, the boy Buck; he sees the public slaughter of a drunk; he hears the vicious plans of murderers on a wrecked steamboat; he spends a large portion of the book in the company of "[Pap's] kind of people"—the fraudulent, thieving

Duke and King who wield brutal power over him, just as his father did. No wonder that when he is alone, whether safe in the Widow's house or hiding from his father, he is so very frightened and frequently suicidal.

If the emotional environment into which Twain places his protagonist is dangerous, then the leading question the novel poses for me is, What does Huck need to live without terror, melancholy and suicidal thoughts? The answer, of course, is Jim. When Huck is among society—whether respectable or deviant, rich or poor—he is alert to and consumed by its deception, its illogic, its scariness. Yet he is depressed by himself and sees nature more often as fearful. But when he and Jim become the only "we," the anxiety is outside, not within. "... we would watch the lonesomeness of the river ... for about an hour ... just solid lonesomeness". Unmanageable terror gives way to a pastoral, idyllic, intimate timelessness minus the hierarchy of age, status or adult control. It has never seemed to me that, in contrast to the entrapment and menace of the shore, the river itself provides this solace. The consolation, the healing properties Huck longs for, is made possible by Jim's active, highly vocal affection. It is in Jim's company that the dread of contemplated nature disappears, that even storms are beautiful and sublime, that real talk—comic, pointed, sad—takes place. Talk so free of lies it produces an aura of restfulness and peace unavailable anywhere else in the novel.

Pleasant as this relationship is, suffused as it is by a lightness they both enjoy and a burden of responsibility both assume, it cannot continue. Knowing the relationship is discontinuous, doomed to separation, is (or used to be) typical of the experience of white/black childhood friendships (mine included), and the cry of inevitable rupture is all the more anguished by being mute. Every reader knows that Jim will be dismissed without explanation at some point; that no enduring adult fraternity will emerge. Anticipating this loss may

Scene from the 1960 film version of the novel. For Huck, Jim is a father-for-free. MGM/ The Kobal Collection.

have led Twain to the over-the-top minstrelization of Jim. Predictable and common as the gross stereotyping of blacks was in nineteenth-century literature, here, nevertheless, Jim's portrait seems unaccountably excessive and glaring in its contradictions—like an ill-made clown suit that cannot hide the man within. Twain's black characters were most certainly based on real people. His nonfiction observations of and comments on "actual" blacks are full of references to their guilelessness, intelligence, creativity, wit, caring, etc. None is portrayed as relentlessly idiotic. Yet Jim is unlike, in many ways, the real people he must have been based on. There may be more than one reason for this extravagance. In addition to accommodating a racist readership, writing Jim so complete a buffoon solves the problem of "missing" him that would have been unacceptable at the novel's end, and helps to solve another problem: how effectively to bury the father figure underneath the minstrel paint. The foregone temporariness of the friendship urges the degradation of Jim (to divert Huck's and our inadvertent sorrow at the close), and minstrelizing him necessitates and exposes an enforced silence on the subject of white fatherhood.

The withholdings at critical moments, which I once took to be deliberate evasions, stumbles even, or a writer's impatience with his or her material, I began to see as otherwise: as entrances, crevices, gaps, seductive invitations flashing the possibility of meaning. Unarticulated eddies that encourage diving into the novel's undertow—the real place where writer captures reader. An excellent example of what is available in this undertow is the way Twain comments on the relationship between the antebellum period in which the narrative takes place and the later period in which the novel was composed. The 1880s saw the collapse of civil rights for blacks as well as the publication of *Huckleberry Finn*. This collapse was an effort to bury the combustible issues Twain raised in his novel. The nation, as well as Tom Sawyer, was deferring Jim's freedom in agonizing play. The cyclical attempts to remove the novel from classrooms extend Jim's captivity on into each generation of readers. . . .

As an abused and homeless child running from a feral male parent, Huck cannot dwell on Jim's confession and regret about parental negligence without precipitating a crisis from which neither he nor the text could recover. Huck's desire for a father who is adviser and trustworthy companion is universal, but he also needs something more: a father whom, unlike his own, he can control. No white man can serve all three functions. If the runaway Huck discovered on the island had been a white convict with protective paternal instincts, none of this would work, for there could be no guarantee of control and no games-playing nonsense concerning his release at the end. Only a black male slave can deliver all Huck desires. Because Jim can be controlled, it becomes possible for

Huck to feel responsible for and to him—but without the onerous burden of lifelong debt that a real father figure would demand. For Huck, Jim is a father-for-free. This delicate, covert and fractious problematic is thus hidden and exposed by litotes and speechlessness, both of which are dramatic ways of begging attention. . . .

As a reader I am relieved to know Pap is no longer a menace to his son's well-being, but Huck does not share my relief. Again the father business is erased. What after all could Huck say? That he is as glad as I am? That would not do. Huck's decency prevents him from taking pleasure in anybody's death. That he is sorry? Wishes his father were alive? Hardly. The whole premise of escape while fearing and feigning death would collapse, and the contradiction would be unacceptable. Instead the crevice widens and beckons reflection on what this long-withheld information means. Any comment at this juncture, positive or negative, would lay bare the white father/white son animosity and harm the prevailing though illicit black father/white son bonding that has already taken place. . . .

Earlier I posed the question, What does Huck need to live without despair and thoughts of suicide? My answer was, Jim. There is another question the novel poses for me: What would it take for Huck to live happily without Jim? That is the problem that gnarls the dissolution of their relationship. The freeing of Jim is withheld, fructified, top-heavy with pain, because without Jim there is no more book, no more story to tell. . . .

The source of my unease reading this amazing, troubling book now seems clear: an imperfect coming to terms with three matters Twain addresses—Huck Finn's estrangement, soleness and morbidity as an outcast child; the disproportionate sadness at the center of Jim's and his relationship; and the secrecy in which Huck's engagement with (rather than escape from) a racist society is necessarily conducted. It is also clear that the rewards of my effort to come to terms have been abundant. My alarm, aroused by Twain's precise rendering of childhood's fear of death and abandonment, remains—as it should. It has been extremely worthwhile slogging through Jim's shame and humiliation to recognize the sadness, the tragic implications at the center of his relationship with Huck. My fury at the maze of deceit, the risk of personal harm that a white child is forced to negotiate in a race-inflected society, is dissipated by the exquisite uses to which Twain puts that maze, that risk.

Yet the larger question, the danger that sifts from the novel's last page, is whether Huck, minus Jim, will be able to stay those three monsters as he enters the "territory." Will that undefined space, so falsely imagined as "open," be free of social chaos, personal morbidity, and further moral complications embedded in adulthood and citizenship? Will it be free not only of nightmare fathers but of dream fathers too?. . .

For a hundred years, the argument that this novel *is* has been identified, reidentified, examined, waged and advanced. What it cannot be is dismissed. It is classic literature, which is to say it heaves, manifests and lasts.

Romanticism, Religion, and Racism

David L. Smith

David L. Smith is the John W. Chandler Professor of English at Williams College. He is a poet, director of the College Arts Endowment, and contributing advisory editor of the journal the Black Scholar.

David L. Smith writes in the following essay that those who are convinced that Adventures of Huckleberry Finn *is a racist novel fail to understand that the book is (except for the works of Herman Melville), "without peer among Euro-American novels for its clear anti-racist stance." Nor do many liberal critics who admire the novel grasp the full revolutionary nature of its attacks on romanticism, religion, and society's idea of blackness—all of which are intertwined. Smith explains the necessity of Twain's use of the "N" word in the novel. He also notes that Twain has created in Jim a repudiation of society's stereotype of black people; Jim is perceptive and intelligent. At the same time, Twain shows the phoniness of romanticism and the hypocrisy of religion that enslaves both blacks and whites.*

In July 1876, exactly one century after the American Declaration of Independence, Mark Twain began writing *Adventures of Huckleberry Finn*, a novel that illustrates trenchantly the social limitations that American "civilization" imposes on individual freedom. The book takes special note of ways in which racism impinges upon the lives of Afro-Americans, even when they are legally "free." It is therefore ironic that *Huckleberry Finn* has often been attacked and even censored as a racist work. I would argue, on the contrary, that except for [Herman] Melville's work, *Huckleberry Finn* is without peer among major Euro-American novels for its explicitly antiracist stance. Those who brand the book racist generally do so without having considered the specific form of racial discourse to which the novel responds. Furthermore, *Huckleberry Finn* offers much more than the typical liberal defenses of "human dignity" and protests against cruelty. Though it contains some such elements, it is more fundamentally a critique of those socially constituted fictions—most notably romanticism, religion, and the concept of "the Negro"—which serve to justify and disguise selfish, cruel, and exploitative behavior. . . .

Twain's Anti-Racist Stance

For obvious reasons, the primary emphasis historically has been on defining "the Negro" as a deviant from Euro-American norms. "Race" in America means white supremacy, and black inferiority, and "the Negro," a socially constituted fiction, is a generalized, one-dimensional surrogate for the historical reality of Afro-American people. It is this reified fiction that Twain attacks in *Huckleberry Finn*.

Twain adopts a strategy of subversion in his attack on race. That is, he focuses on a number of commonplaces associated with "the Negro" and then systematically dramatizes their inadequacy. He uses the term "nigger," and he shows Jim engaging in superstitious behavior. Yet he portrays Jim as a compassionate, shrewd, thoughtful, self-sacrificing, and even wise man. . . . Jim is cautious, he gives excellent advice, he suffers persistent anguish over separation from his wife and children, and he even sacrifices his own sleep so that Huck may rest. Jim, in short, exhibits all the qualities that "the Negro" supposedly lacks. Twain's conclusions do more than merely subvert the justifications of slavery, which was already long since abolished. Twain began his book during the final disintegration of Reconstruction, and his satire on antebellum [pre–Civil War] southern bigotry is also an implicit response to the Negrophobic climate of the post-Reconstruction era. It is troubling, therefore, that so many readers have completely misunderstood Twain's subtle attack on racism.

Racist Language

Twain's use of the term "nigger" has provoked some readers to reject the novel. As one of the most offensive words in our vocabulary, "nigger" remains heavily shrouded in taboo. A careful assessment of this term within the context of American racial discourse, however, will allow us to understand the particular way in which the author uses it. If we attend closely to Twain's use of the word, we may find in it not just a trigger to outrage but, more important, a means of understanding the precise nature of American racism and Mark Twain's attack on it. . . .

The View of "the Negro"

The exchange between Huck and Aunt Sally reveals a great deal about how racial discourse operates. Its function is to promulgate a conception of "the Negro" as a subhuman and expendable creature who is by definition feeble-minded, immoral, lazy, and superstitious. One crucial purpose of this social fiction is to justify the abuse and exploitation of Afro-American people by substituting the essentialist fiction of "Negroism" for the actual character of individual Afro-Americans. Hence, in racial discourse every Afro-American becomes just another instance of "the Negro"—just another "nigger." Twain recognizes this invidious tendency of race thinking, however, and he takes every opportunity to expose the mismatch between racial abstractions and real human beings. . . .

A reader who objects to the word "nigger" might still insist that Twain could have avoided using it. But it is difficult to imagine how Twain could have debunked a discourse without using the specific terms of that discourse. Even when Twain was writing his book, "nigger" was universally recognized as an insulting, demeaning word. According to Stuart Berg Flexner, "Negro" was generally pronounced "nigger" until about 1825, at which time abolitionists began objecting to that term. They preferred "colored person" or "person of color." . . . The objections to "nigger," then, are not a consequence of the modern sensibility but had been common for a half century before *Huckleberry Finn* was published. The specific function of this term in the book, however, is neither to offend nor merely to provide linguistic authenticity. Much more importantly, it establishes a context against which Jim's specific virtues may emerge as explicit refutations of racist presuppositions. . . .

As a serious critic of American society, Twain recognized that racial discourse depends upon the deployment of a system of stereotypes which constitute "the Negro" as fundamentally different from and inferior to Euro-Americans. As with his handling of "nigger," Twain's strategy with racial stereotypes is to elaborate them in order to undermine them. To be sure, those critics are correct who have argued that Twain uses this narrative to reveal Jim's humanity. Jim, however, is just one individual. Twain uses the narrative to expose the cruelty and hollowness of that racial discourse which exists only to obscure the humanity of *all* Afro-American people. . . .

Jim's Intelligence

Jim emerges as an astute and sensitive observer of human behavior, both in his comments regarding Pap and in his subtle remarks to Huck. Jim clearly possesses a subtlety and intelligence which "the Negro" allegedly lacks. Twain makes this point more clearly in the debate scene in chapter 14. True enough, most of this debate is, as several critics have noted, conventional minstrel-show banter. Nevertheless, Jim demon-

strates impressive reasoning abilities, despite his factual ignorance. For instance, in their argument over "Poly-voo-franzy,"
Huck makes a category error by implying that the difference
between languages is analogous to the difference between human language and cat language. While Jim's response—that a
man should talk like a man—betrays his ignorance of cultural
diversity, his argument is otherwise perceptive and structurally
sound. The humor in Huck's conclusion, "you can't learn a
nigger to argue," arises precisely from our recognition that
Jim's argument is better than Huck's.

Throughout the novel Twain presents Jim in ways which
render ludicrous the conventional wisdom about "Negro character." As an intelligent, sensitive, wily, and considerate individual, Jim demonstrates that race provides no useful index of
character. While that point may seem obvious to contemporary readers, it is a point rarely made by nineteenth-century
Euro-American novelists.... By presenting us with a series of
glimpses which penetrate the "Negro" exterior and reveal the
person beneath it, Twain debunks American racial discourse.
For racial discourse maintains that the "Negro" exterior is all
that a Negro really has.

This insight in itself is a notable accomplishment. Twain,
however, did not view racism as an isolated phenomenon, and
his effort to place racism within the context of other cultural
traditions produced the most problematic aspect of his novel.
For it is in the final chapters—the Tom Sawyer section—
which most critics consider the weakest part of the book, that
Twain links his criticisms of slavery and southern romanticism, condemning the cruelties that both of these traditions
entail....

Organized Religion

Huck makes what is obviously the morally correct decision,
but his doing so represents more than simply a liberal choice
of conscience over social convention. Twain explicitly makes

Huck's choice a sharp attack on the southern church. Huck scolds himself: "There was the Sunday school, you could a gone to it; and if you'd a done it they'd a learnt you, there, that people that acts as I'd been acting about that nigger goes to everlasting fire". Yet despite Huck's anxiety, he transcends the moral limitations of his time and place. By the time Twain wrote these words, more than twenty years of national strife, including the Civil War and Reconstruction, had established Huck's conclusion regarding slavery as a dominant national consensus; not even reactionary southerners advocated a reinstitution of slavery. But since the pre–Civil War southern church taught that slavery was God's will, Huck's decision flatly repudiates the church's teachings regarding slavery. And implicitly, it also repudiates the church as an institution by suggesting that the church functions to undermine, not to encourage, a reliance on one's conscience. To define "Negroes" as subhuman removes them from moral consideration and therefore justifies their callous exploitation. . . .

Ultimately, *Huckleberry Finn* renders a harsh judgment on American society. Freedom from slavery, the novel implies, is not freedom from gratuitous cruelty; and racism, like romanticism, is finally just an elaborate justification which the adult counterparts of Tom Sawyer use to facilitate their exploitation and abuse of other human beings. Tom feels guilty, with good reason, for having exploited Jim, but his final gesture of paying Jim off is less an insult to Jim than it is Twain's commentary on Tom himself. . . .

"Getting" *Huckleberry Finn*

Given the subtlety of Mark Twain's approach; it is not surprising that most of his contemporaries misunderstood or simply ignored the novel's demystification of race. Despite their patriotic rhetoric, they, like Pap, were unprepared to take seriously the implications of "freedom, justice, and equality." . . . Yet racial discourse flatly contradicts and ultimately renders hypocritical the egalitarian claims of liberal democracy. The heart of Twain's message to us is that an honest person must reject one or the other. But hypocrisy, not honesty, is our norm. Many of us continue to assert both racial distinction and liberal values simultaneously. If we, a century later, continue to be confused about *Adventures of Huckleberry Finn*, perhaps it is because we remain more deeply committed to both racial discourse and a self-deluding optimism than we care to admit.

Social Issues in Literature

CHAPTER 3

Issues of Race in the Twenty-First Century

Some Children Left Behind

Christopher Knaus

Christopher Knaus, associate professor of educational leadership at California State University–East Bay, is the author of Race, Racism, and Multiraciality in American Education.

Many educators have found serious flaws in the George W. Bush administration initiative called No Child Left Behind (NCLB), with its emphasis on standardized testing and superficial evaluation of schools. In the following viewpoint, Christopher Knaus claims that NCLB has created racial inequalities and segregation in public schools. The program is focused on identifying underachieving schools, most of which are black, rather than identifying the reasons behind these failures, Knaus contends. These reasons include having fewer accessible parents, a cultural history of underachievement, language barriers, and family income. The author maintains that by ignoring this resegregation of schools, the government has negatively affected the performance of African American students. Knaus suggests ways of addressing racial inequality and failure in schools. One of the most important, he argues, is creating a broader, more relevant curriculum, including art, music, social studies, speech, and biology, and broadening the tools for assessment to include oral exams, problem solving, and portfolios.

This article examines the impact of No Child Left Behind (NCLB) on educational experiences and opportunities for African-American children. Despite NCLB, public schools have continued to fail African Americans through separate and unequal educational opportunities, partially because the focus on educating African-American children well has not been legislated or mandated.

Christopher Knaus, "Still Segregated, Still Unequal: Analyzing the Impact of No Child Left Behind on African American Students," in *The State of Black America 2007*, New York: National Urban League, 2007, pp. 1005–113. Copyright © 2007, National Urban League. All rights reserved. Reproduced by permission.

Inequalities

In focusing on measuring the outcomes of racial inequalities (such as the achievement gap), NCLB avoids addressing fundamental inequalities in schooling and fails to expose the causes of such inequalities. NCLB advocates for teaching to bare minimums rather than meaningfully educating African-American students. As African Americans continue to be punished for the failures of their schools, NCLB has continued a separate and unequal educational system while shifting the debate from unequal schools to how to measure such schools. . . .

Ignoring Causes

Aligning the curriculum with such narrow standards ignores issues students face daily, including a context of violence, fewer accessible parents, fewer parents who have successfully navigated schooling, and historical (under) achievement levels of the student population, all of which require enhancing, rather than restricting, opportunities to learn. These conditions are precisely what limit many African-American students' willingness to engage in schools. In a national context where some estimates suggest that one of two African-American students drops out before graduation, further narrowing a curriculum many students already find irrelevant is hardly an incentive to stay in school. Furthermore, rather than conceive of schools as working in conjunction with other public service agencies (such as social work, juvenile justice, welfare, health, and employment sectors), NCLB operates in isolation from social services. Yet researchers have often demonstrated that educational achievement is directly tied to the social conditions in which students live. NCLB ignores how the surrounding community, parental income and education levels, language and cultural barriers, teacher awareness of student cultural context, and pedagogical approaches influence academic engagement of all students. . . .

Because NCLB ignores the social context that shapes opportunity for many African American youth, it shifts the conversation about educational equity away from what really matters. Federal assessments are not required for critical thinking, art, history, biology, or anything specifically related to participating in democratic society as a creative or independent thinker, and NCLB provides incentives to eliminate such curricula from "failing" schools. Increasingly absent from low-income urban schools across the country are creative, flexible curricula that allow students to express themselves outside the arena of what may be on a test. NCLB ultimately requires basic, rote educational strategies for failing schools; a requirement that would be rejected by elite schools as an inadequate method for engaging students in higher-level critical thinking skills valued by colleges and employers alike.

Resegregation

African Americans often attend urban schools that are woefully inadequate when compared to schools attended by the majority of white students. While such race-based segregation is not new, it is increasing. Since desegregation efforts have all but formally ended, the percentage of African Americans attending predominantly minority schools nationwide has steadily increased. In 2003, 73 percent of African-American students attended a predominantly minority school, and 38 percent of African Americans attended a school that is over 90 percent minority (in 1991, those numbers were 66 percent and 34 percent). In 2005, 71 percent of African-American students attended a predominantly minority school, whereas only 11 percent of white students did. This racial segregation is tied to increasing poverty—in 1996, the average African-American student attended a school where at least 43 percent of its students were poor. In 2002, that number increased to 49 percent. Nationwide, 48 percent of African-American students attend schools where over 75 percent of the students are eligible for free or reduced price lunch, and 72 percent attend schools where over 51 percent of the students are eligible. Segregation negatively impacts student achievement. One recent study shows that African-American students in Florida who attend segregated schools perform lower on state tests than African-American students in non-segregated schools, even after controlling for teacher quality, class size, and poverty levels. . . .

Students not meeting proficiency are often isolated from students who are meeting proficiency and additional federal funds are often spent on after school or pull-out programs for failing minority students. While data is not readily available on the percentages of African-American students being tracked into "support" structures (that segregate), educators note that many are pushed into alternative education systems (another segregated population). Therefore, instead of addressing segregation of our public schools, NCLB punishes students who attend segregated low-income minority schools. . . .

Teacher Quality

NCLB requires a "highly qualified" teacher in every classroom, but how this relates to effectiveness at teaching African-American students is under question. What is certain is that high-poverty and high-minority schools have much lower proportions of "highly qualified" teachers. For example, one recent study found significant gaps between classes taught by highly qualified teachers in high- and low-poverty schools in 2003–04. In California, that gap was particularly extensive—40 percent of core classes were taught by highly qualified teachers in high-poverty schools, while 60 percent were taught by highly qualified teachers in low-poverty schools. . . .

Addressing Racial Inequality

Given the lack of improvement in the achievement gap, according to its own measures, NCLB appears to have failed in its first five years. NCLB lacks the capacity to prepare African-

The "No Child Left Behind" policy fails to address fundamental inequalities in schooling. Image copyright Orange Line Media, 2009. Used under license from Shutterstock.com.

American students for critical engagement in shaping democratic society, encourages segregated schools, pushes students out of mainstream schools, narrows a curriculum that many African-American students already find alienating, and ignores high drop out rates. Despite the rhetoric of NCLB, schools in which a majority of students are African American are still in disrepair, are still staffed by less experienced teachers, and generally do not provide a college preparatory curriculum. But NCLB has provided a forum through which advocates of African-American students can offer meaningful policy recommendations for strengthening educational opportunities and improving educational outcomes for African-American students. Current policy conversation should concentrate on three primary concerns:

- Expanding definitions of academic skills beyond math and reading. A central pillar of NCLB is relevant research; however, much of the research about the skills needed for meaningful participation in democratic society is being ignored. Important subjects such as art, music, history, biology, speech, and social studies must be included in the fabric of schooling.

- Reengaging African-American students in the educational process. Conversations with students, educators, policy makers, and communities about how to best educate African-American students should be informed by research on culturally relevant and responsive pedagogy, curricula, and school structures.

- Expansion of assessment to include multiple measures of academic success. Research has shown that in order for assessment to effectively guide school efforts, it must reflect a wide range of student skills and provide a foundation from which to teach. Multiple measures include portfolios, teacher assessments, problem solving, diagnostic feedback for students, project management, essays, oral exams, and public performance.

On Race: Toward a More Perfect Union

Barack Obama

Barack Obama became the first African American president of the United States in 2009.

As a candidate, Barack Obama delivered this address after racial issues intruded into the 2008 presidential campaign. It is a hopeful speech about the prospect of unity between blacks and whites in the United States. He begins by pointing out that the United States Constitution was marred by its failure to abolish the slave trade. With the abolition of slavery and the civil rights movement of the twentieth century, some of the nation's injustices and inequality began to be addressed, but the impediments to reaching the American Dream continued in segregated schools, income gaps between blacks and whites, and inequities in neighborhood services. Black citizens's memories of humiliation bred racial hatred on the part of blacks, and governmental attempts to correct these inequities with affirmative action has fired white anger. But, at this time, he asserts, the country should come together to address national problems that affect black and white children, Asian and Hispanic children, and Native American children—their educations, health care, and jobs.

"We the people, in order to form a more perfect union."

Two hundred and twenty-one years ago, in a hall that still stands across the street, a group of men gathered and, with these simple words, launched America's improbable experiment in democracy. Farmers and scholars; statesmen and pa-

Barack Obama, "Remarks of Senator Barack Obama, A More Perfect Union, Constitution Center, Philadelphia, Pennsylvania," March 18, 2008.

triots who had traveled across an ocean to escape tyranny and persecution finally made real their declaration of independence at a Philadelphia convention that lasted through the spring of 1787.

The document they produced was eventually signed but ultimately unfinished. It was stained by this nation's original sin of slavery, a question that divided the colonies and brought the convention to a stalemate until the founders chose to allow the slave trade to continue for at least twenty more years, and to leave any final resolution to future generations.

Ideal of Equality Is Not Reality

Of course, the answer to the slavery question was already embedded within our Constitution—a Constitution that had at its very core the ideal of equal citizenship under the law; a Constitution that promised its people liberty, and justice, and a union that could be and should be perfected over time.

And yet words on a parchment would not be enough to deliver slaves from bondage, or provide men and women of every color and creed their full rights and obligations as citizens of the United States. What would be needed were Americans in successive generations who were willing to do their part—through protests and struggle, on the streets and in the courts, through a civil war and civil disobedience and always at great risk—to narrow that gap between the promise of our ideals and the reality of their time.

This was one of the tasks we set forth at the beginning of this campaign—to continue the long march of those who came before us, a march for a more just, more equal, more free, more caring and more prosperous America. I chose to run for the presidency at this moment in history because I believe deeply that we cannot solve the challenges of our time unless we solve them together—unless we perfect our union by understanding that we may have different stories, but we hold common hopes; that we may not look the same and we may not have come from the same place, but we all want to move in the same direction—towards a better future for our children and our grandchildren.

This belief comes from my unyielding faith in the decency and generosity of the American people. But it also comes from my own American story.

I am the son of a black man from Kenya and a white woman from Kansas. I was raised with the help of a white grandfather who survived a Depression to serve in Patton's Army during World War II and a white grandmother who worked on a bomber assembly line at Fort Leavenworth while he was overseas. I've gone to some of the best schools in America and lived in one of the world's poorest nations. I am married to a black American who carries within her the blood of slaves and slaveowners—an inheritance we pass on to our two precious daughters. I have brothers, sisters, nieces, nephews, uncles and cousins, of every race and every hue, scattered across three continents, and for as long as I live, I will never forget that in no other country on Earth is my story even possible.

It's a story that hasn't made me the most conventional candidate. But it is a story that has seared into my genetic makeup the idea that this nation is more than the sum of its parts—that out of many, we are truly one.

Racial Unity and Division

Throughout the first year of this campaign, against all predictions to the contrary, we saw how hungry the American people were for this message of unity. Despite the temptation to view my candidacy through a purely racial lens, we won commanding victories in states with some of the whitest populations in the country. In South Carolina, where the Confederate Flag still flies, we built a powerful coalition of African Americans and white Americans.

This is not to say that race has not been an issue in the campaign. At various stages in the campaign, some commentators have deemed me either "too black" or "not black enough." We saw racial tensions bubble to the surface during the week before the South Carolina primary. The press has scoured every exit poll for the latest evidence of racial polarization, not just in terms of white and black, but black and brown as well.

Racial Discrimination

The fact is that the comments that have been made and the issues that have surfaced over the last few weeks reflect the complexities of race in this country that we've never really worked through—a part of our union that we have yet to perfect. And if we walk away now, if we simply retreat into our respective corners, we will never be able to come together and solve challenges like health care, or education, or the need to find good jobs for every American.

Understanding this reality requires a reminder of how we arrived at this point. As William Faulkner once wrote, "The past isn't dead and buried. In fact, it isn't even past." We do not need to recite here the history of racial injustice in this country. But we do need to remind ourselves that so many of the disparities that exist in the African-American community today can be directly traced to inequalities passed on from an earlier generation that suffered under the brutal legacy of slavery and Jim Crow.

Segregated schools were, and are, inferior schools; we still haven't fixed them, fifty years after *Brown v. Board of Education*, and the inferior education they provided, then and now, helps explain the pervasive achievement gap between today's black and white students.

Legalized discrimination—where blacks were prevented, often through violence, from owning property, or loans were not granted to African-American business owners, or black homeowners could not access FHA [Federal Housing Administration] mortgages, or blacks were excluded from unions, or the police force, or fire departments—meant that black families could not amass any meaningful wealth to bequeath to future generations. That history helps explain the wealth and income gap between black and white, and the concentrated pockets of poverty that persist in so many of today's urban and rural communities.

A lack of economic opportunity among black men, and the shame and frustration that came from not being able to provide for one's family, contributed to the erosion of black families—a problem that welfare policies for many years may have worsened. And the lack of basic services in so many urban black neighborhoods—parks for kids to play in, police walking the beat, regular garbage pick-up and building code enforcement—all helped create a cycle of violence, blight and neglect that continue to haunt us. . . .

But for all those who scratched and clawed their way to get a piece of the American Dream, there were many who didn't make it—those who were ultimately defeated, in one way or another, by discrimination. That legacy of defeat was passed on to future generations—those young men and, increasingly, young women whom we see standing on street corners or languishing in our prisons, without hope or prospects for the future. Even for those blacks who did make it, questions of race, and racism, continue to define their worldview in fundamental ways. . . . The memories of humiliation and doubt and fear have not gone away; nor has the anger and the bitterness of those years. That anger may not get expressed in public, in front of white co-workers or white friends. But it does find voice in the barbershop or around the kitchen table. At times, that anger is exploited by politicians, to gin up votes along racial lines, or to make up for a politician's own failings. . . .

Barack Obama, the first African American president of the United States, encourages unity of all people in the spirit of Abraham Lincoln. Scott J. Ferrell/Congressional Quarterly/ Getty Images.

Racial Anger of Blacks and Whites

In fact, a similar anger exists within segments of the white community. Most working- and middle-class white Americans don't feel that they have been particularly privileged by their race. Their experience is the immigrant experience—as far as they're concerned, no one's handed them anything, they've built it from scratch. They've worked hard all their lives, many times only to see their jobs shipped overseas or their pension dumped after a lifetime of labor. They are anxious about their futures, and feel their dreams slipping away; in an era of stagnant wages and global competition, opportunity comes to be seen as a zero sum game, in which your dreams come at my expense. So when they are told to bus their children to a school across town; when they hear that an African American is getting an advantage in landing a good job or a spot in a good college because of an injustice that they themselves never committed; when they're told that their fears about crime in urban neighborhoods are somehow prejudiced, resentment builds over time.

Like the anger within the black community, these resentments aren't always expressed in polite company. But they have helped shape the political landscape for at least a generation. Anger over welfare and affirmative action helped forge the Reagan Coalition. Politicians routinely exploited fears of crime for their own electoral ends. Talk show hosts and conservative commentators built entire careers unmasking bogus claims of racism while dismissing legitimate discussions of racial injustice and inequality as mere political correctness or reverse racism.

Just as black anger often proved counterproductive, so have these white resentments distracted attention from the real culprits of the middle class squeeze—a corporate culture rife with inside dealing, questionable accounting practices, and short-term greed; a Washington dominated by lobbyists and special interests; economic policies that favor the few over the many. And yet, to wish away the resentments of white Americans, to label them as misguided or even racist, without recognizing they are grounded in legitimate concerns—this too widens the racial divide, and blocks the path to understanding. . . .

At this moment, in this election, we can come together and say, "Not this time". This time we want to talk about the crumbling schools that are stealing the future of black children and white children and Asian children and Hispanic children and Native American children. This time we want to reject the cynicism that tells us that these kids can't learn; that those kids who don't look like us are somebody else's problem. The children of America are not those kids, they are our kids, and we will not let them fall behind in a 21st century economy. Not this time.

This time we want to talk about how the lines in the Emergency Room are filled with whites and blacks and Hispanics who do not have health care; who don't have the power on their own to overcome the special interests in Washington, but who can take them on if we do it together.

This time we want to talk about the shuttered mills that once provided a decent life for men and women of every race, and the homes for sale that once belonged to Americans from every religion, every region, every walk of life. This time we want to talk about the fact that the real problem is not that someone who doesn't look like you might take your job; it's that the corporation you work for will ship it overseas for nothing more than a profit.

This time we want to talk about the men and women of every color and creed who serve together, and fight together, and bleed together under the same proud flag. We want to talk about how to bring them home from a war that never should've been authorized and never should've been waged, and we want to talk about how we'll show our patriotism by caring for them, and their families, and giving them the benefits they have earned.

I would not be running for President if I didn't believe with all my heart that this is what the vast majority of Americans want for this country. This union may never be perfect, but generation after generation has shown that it can always be perfected. And today, whenever I find myself feeling doubtful or cynical about this possibility, what gives me the most hope is the next generation—the young people whose attitudes and beliefs and openness to change have already made history in this election.

Racism on the Campaign Trail

Kevin Merida

Kevin Merida, associate editor of the Washington Post, *was named Journalist of the Year by the National Association of Black Journalists in 2000.*

On November 4, 2008, America chose its first African American president by a comfortable margin. But this exhilarating event was marked by occasions of racism both before and after the election. While Barack Obama was drawing widely enthusiastic crowds in numbers rarely seen before in a presidential campaign, his volunteers in the field, or those on the phones, were encountering vicious antiblack sentiments. Some of the people stated frankly that they'd never vote for a black person. Some of the bigotry went beyond rhetoric: a plate-glass window was smashed; other windows were spray painted with racial epithets; an American flag was stolen; and there were numerous bomb threats. Despite Obama's success, his volunteers have been enraged and frustrated by the racism they encountered throughout the campaign.

Danielle Ross was alone in an empty room at the Obama campaign headquarters in Kokomo, Ind., a cellphone in one hand, a voter call list in the other. She was stretched out on the carpeted floor wearing laceless sky-blue Converses, stories from the trail on her mind.

Racism During the Campaign

It was the day before Indiana's primary, and she had just been chased by dogs while canvassing in a Kokomo suburb. But that was not the worst thing to occur since she postponed her

Kevin Merida, "Racist Incidents Give Some Obama Campaigners Pause," *The Washington Post*, May 13, 2008, p. A01. Copyright © 2008, *The Washington Post*. Reprinted with permission.

sophomore year at Middle Tennessee State University, in part to hopscotch America stumping for Barack Obama.

Here's the worst: In Muncie, a factory town in the east-central part of Indiana, Ross and her cohorts were soliciting support for Obama at malls, on street corners and in a Wal-Mart parking lot, and they ran into "a horrible response," as Ross put it, a level of anti-black sentiment that none of them had anticipated.

"The first person I encountered was like, 'I'll never vote for a black person,'" recalled Ross, who is white and just turned 20. "People just weren't receptive."

For all the hope and excitement Obama's candidacy is generating, some of his field workers, phone-bank volunteers and campaign surrogates are encountering a raw racism and hostility that have gone largely unnoticed—and unreported—this election season. Doors have been slammed in their faces. They've been called racially derogatory names (including the white volunteers). And they've endured malicious rants and ugly stereotyping from people who can't fathom that the senator from Illinois could become the first African American president.

A Contrast to Adoring Crowds

The contrast between the large, adoring crowds Obama draws at public events and the gritty street-level work to win votes is stark. The candidate is largely insulated from the mean-spiritedness that some of his foot soldiers deal with away from the media spotlight.

Victoria Switzer, a retired social studies teacher, was on phone-bank duty one night during the Pennsylvania primary campaign. One night was all she could take: "It wasn't pretty." She made 60 calls to prospective voters in Susquehanna County, her home county, which is 98 percent white. The responses were dispiriting. One caller, Switzer remembers, said he couldn't possibly vote for Obama and concluded: "Hang that darky from a tree!"

Documentary filmmaker Rory Kennedy, the daughter of the late Robert F. Kennedy, said she, too, came across "a lot of racism" when campaigning for Obama in Pennsylvania. One Pittsburgh union organizer told her he would not vote for Obama because he is black, and a white voter, she said, offered this frank reason for not backing Obama: "White people look out for white people, and black people look out for black people."

Positive and Negative Responses

Obama campaign officials say such incidents are isolated, that the experience of most volunteers and staffers has been overwhelmingly positive.

The campaign released this statement in response to questions about encounters with racism: "After campaigning for 15 months in nearly all 50 states, Barack Obama and our entire campaign have been nothing but impressed and encouraged by the core decency, kindness, and generosity of Americans from all walks of life. The last year has only reinforced Senator Obama's view that this country is not as divided as our politics suggest."

Campaign field work can be an exercise in confronting the fears, anxieties and prejudices of voters. Veterans of the civil rights movement know what this feels like, as do those who have been involved in battles over busing, immigration or abortion. But through the Obama campaign, some young people are having their first experience joining a cause and meeting cruel reaction.

On Election Day in Kokomo, a group of black high school students were holding up Obama signs along U.S. 31, a major thoroughfare. As drivers cruised by, a number of them rolled down their windows and yelled out a common racial slur for African Americans, according to Obama campaign staffers.

Frederick Murrell, a black Kokomo High School senior, was not there but heard what happened. He was more disappointed than surprised. During his own canvassing for Obama, Murrell said, he had "a lot of doors slammed" in his face. But taunting teenagers on a busy commercial strip in broad daylight? "I was very shocked at first," Murrell said. "Then again, I wasn't, because we have a lot of racism here."

Bigotry Beyond Words

The bigotry has gone beyond words. In Vincennes, the Obama campaign office was vandalized at 2 a.m. on the eve of the primary, according to police. A large plate-glass window was smashed, an American flag stolen. Other windows were spray-painted with references to Obama's controversial former pastor, the Rev. Jeremiah Wright, and other political messages: "Hamas votes BHO" and "We don't cling to guns or religion. Goddamn Wright."

Ray McCormick was notified of the incident at about 2:45 a.m. A farmer and conservationist, McCormick had erected a giant billboard on a major highway on behalf of Farmers for Obama. He also was housing the Obama campaign worker manning the office. When McCormick arrived at the office, about two hours before he was due out of bed to plant corn, he grabbed his camera and wanted to alert the media. "I thought, this is a big deal." But he was told Obama campaign officials didn't want to make a big deal of the incident. McCormick took photos anyway and distributed some.

"The pictures represent what we are breaking through and overcoming," he said. As McCormick, who is white, sees it, Obama is succeeding despite these incidents. Later, there would be bomb threats to three Obama campaign offices in Indiana, including the one in Vincennes, according to campaign sources.

Safety Issues

Obama has not spoken much about racism during this campaign. He has sought to emphasize connections among Americans rather than divisions. He shrugged off safety concerns that led to early Secret Service protection and has told black senior citizens who worry that racists will do him harm: Don't fret. Earlier in the campaign, a 68-year-old woman in Carson City, Nev., voiced concern that the country was not ready to elect an African American president.

"Will there be some folks who probably won't vote for me because I am black? Of course," Obama said, "just like there may be somebody who won't vote for Hillary because she's a woman or wouldn't vote for John Edwards because they don't like his accent. But the question is, 'Can we get a majority of the American people to give us a fair hearing?'"

Evidence of Overcoming Racism

Obama has won 30 of 50 Democratic contests so far, the kind of nationwide electoral triumph no black candidate has ever realized. That he is on the brink of capturing the Democratic nomination, some say, is a testament to how far the country has progressed in overcoming racism and evidence of Obama's skill at bridging divides.

Obama has won five of 12 primaries in which black voters made up less than 10 percent of the electorate, and caucuses in states such as Idaho and Wyoming that are overwhelmingly white. But exit polls show he has struggled to attract white voters who didn't attend college and earn less than $50,000 a year. . . .

For the most part, Obama campaign workers say, the 2008 election cycle has been exhilarating. On the ground, the Obama campaign is being driven by youngsters, many of whom are imbued with an optimism undeterred by racial intolerance. "We've grown up in a different world," says Danielle Ross. Field offices are staffed by 20-somethings who hold positions—state director, regional field director, field organizer—that are typically off limits to newcomers to presidential politics.

Racist Lies

Gillian Bergeron, 23, was in charge of a five-county regional operation in northeastern Pennsylvania. The oldest member of her team was 27. At Scranton's annual Saint Patrick's Day parade, some of the green Obama signs distributed by staffers were burned along the parade route. That was the first signal that this wasn't exactly Obama country. There would be others.

In a letter to the editor published in a local paper, Tunkhannock Borough Mayor Norm Ball explained his support of Hillary Clinton this way: "Barack Hussein Obama and all of his talk will do nothing for our country. There is so much that people don't know about his upbringing in the Muslim world. His stepfather was a radical Muslim and the ranting of his minister against the white America, you can't convince me that some of that didn't rub off on him.

"No, I want a president that will salute our flag, and put their hand on the Bible when they take the oath of office."

Obama's campaign workers have grown wearily accustomed to the lies about the candidate's supposed radical Muslim ties and lack of patriotism. But they are sometimes astonished when public officials such as Ball or others representing the campaign of their opponent traffic in these falsehoods.

Karen Seifert, a volunteer from New York, was outside of the largest polling location in Lackawanna County, Pa., on primary day when she was pressed by a Clinton volunteer to explain her backing of Obama. "I trust him," Seifert replied. According to Seifert, the woman pointed to Obama's face on Seifert's T-shirt and said: "He's a half-breed and he's a Muslim. How can you trust that?"

Pollsters have found it difficult to accurately measure racial attitudes, as some voters are unwilling to acknowledge the role that race plays in their thinking. But some are not. Susan Dzimian, a Clinton supporter who owns residential properties, said outside a polling location in Kokomo that race was a factor in how she viewed Obama. "I think if it was somebody other than him, I'd accept it," she said of a black candidate. "If Colin Powell had run, I would be willing to accept him."

Working-Class Whites

The previous evening, Dondra Ewing was driving the neighborhoods of Kokomo, looking to turn around voters like Dzimian. Ewing, 47, is a chain-smoking middle school guidance counselor, a black single mother of two and one of the most fiercely vigilant Obama volunteers in Kokomo, which was once a Ku Klux Klan stronghold. On July 4, 1923, Kokomo hosted the largest Klan gathering in history—an estimated 200,000 followers flocked to a local park. But these are not the 1920s, and Ewing believes she can persuade anybody to back Obama. Her mother, after all, was the first African American elected at-large to the school board in a community that is 10 percent black.

Kokomo, population 46,000, is another hard-hit Midwestern industrial town stung by layoffs. Longtimers wistfully remember the glory years of Continental Steel and speak mournfully about the jobs shipped overseas. Kokomo Sanitary Pottery, which made bathroom sinks and toilets, shut down a couple of months ago and took with it 150 jobs.

Aaron Roe, 23, was mowing lawns at a local cemetery recently, lamenting his $8-an-hour job with no benefits. He had earned a community college degree as an industrial electrician, but learned there was no electrical work to be found for someone with his experience, which is to say none. Politics wasn't on his mind; frustration was. If he were to vote, it would not be for Obama, he said. "I just got a funny feeling about him," Roe said, a feeling he couldn't specify, except to say race wasn't a part of it. "Race ain't nothing," said Roe, who is white. "It's how they're going to help the country."

The Aaron Roes are exactly who Dondra Ewing was after: people with funny feelings.

At the Bradford Run Apartments, she found Robert Cox, a retiree who spent 30 years working for an electronics manufacturer making computer chips. He was in his suspenders, grilling shish kebab, which he had never eaten. "Something new," Cox said, recommended by his son who was visiting from Colorado.

Ewing was selling him hard on Obama. "There are more than two families that can run the United States of America," she said, "and their names aren't Bush and Clinton."

"Yeah, I know, I know," Cox said, remaining noncommittal.

He opened the grill and peeked at the kebabs. "It's not his race, because I got real good friends and all that," Cox continued. "If anything would keep him from getting elected, it would be his name. It might turn off some older people."

Like him?

"No, older than me," said Cox, 66.

Ewing kept talking, until finally Cox said, "Probably Obama," when asked directly how he would vote.

As she walked away, Ewing said: "I think we got him."

But truthfully, she wasn't feeling so sure.

Still Slavery, Still Racism

Larry Lipman

Larry Lipman is the Palm Beach Post *bureau chief in the paper's Washington bureau and former president of the National Press Club.*

The following article by Larry Lipman is pertinent to Adventures of Huckleberry Finn *because it reports the existence of slavery in 2008 in the United States and because that slavery is race based. In these cases, however, the workers are primarily Latin Americans. Testimony was given by a county sheriff of Collier County, Florida, to a United States Senate subcommittee that tomato workers were being held under conditions of slavery. The vice president of the Florida Tomato Growers Exchange disputed the sheriff's testimony. Seven cases of slavery of Latino workers have been prosecuted in Florida. This, reported a workers's advocate, was just the tip of the iceberg. Slavery is perpetrated by growers in the form of human trafficking, involuntary servitude through violence, threats against families—even in Latin America—perpetually accruing debt, low salaries, and high charges for living expenses.*

Slavery exists in the tomato fields of Florida, a U.S. Senate committee was told today.

"Today's form of slavery does not bear the overt nature of pre-Civil War society, but it is nonetheless heinous and reprehensible," Collier County Sheriff's Detective Charlie Frost told Democratic members of the Senate Health, Education, Labor and Pension Committee. No Republicans attended the hearing.

But Reginald L. Brown, executive vice president of the Florida Tomato Growers Exchange, denied slavery exists in the commercial tomato industry. He said isolated cases have occurred among private growers.

"Florida's tomato growers abhor and condemn slavery," Brown said. "We are on the same side on this issue."

Committee members, however, expressed skepticism about the growers' willingness to police their members and said the industry appears to foster low wages and the exploitation of migrant workers.

At the conclusion of the two-hour hearing, Brown reluctantly agreed the exchange would cooperate if the committee requested a Government Accountability Office study of conditions among tomato workers. But Brown said he could not guarantee the individual companies that make up the exchange would cooperate.

The Senate hearing focused on the living and working conditions facing thousands of migrant tomato pickers, their rate of pay, and the industry's refusal to implement agreements by major restaurant chains to pay workers an additional penny a pound for harvested tomatoes.

Lucas Benitez, a co-founder of the Coalition of Immokalee Workers, told the panel that tomato pickers are regularly abused, harassed, intimidated and kept so deeply in debt that they are virtually in bondage. Benitez said female pickers are additionally subjected to sexual harassment and abuse. ·

"The seven cases of modern slavery that have been uncovered in the fields of Florida are just the tip of the iceberg," Benitez said, referring to federal cases in the past decade.

Frost, the Collier County detective, said slavery was the same as human trafficking, but that loopholes in state and federal law make it difficult to bring cases against those who benefit from the system. Frost said the large tomato companies shield themselves from prosecution by hiring subcontractors, who are responsible for human trafficking.

Farmworkers in Florida's tomato fields are appealing to Florida government for improved conditions and more humane relationships with workers. AP Images.

Workers are held in "involuntary servitude" through threats and actual violence against them and their families—often in Latin America—and in a system of "perpetually accruing debt," in which they are overcharged for housing, food, water and transportation, he said

"Almost certainly, it's going on right now," Frost said.

Brown rejected the claim.

"We are paying fair wages and we're paying our workers fairly," Brown said, arguing that if workers were being exploited they would not return voluntarily year after year to work in Florida's tomato fields.

Roy Reyna, a former farm worker who now is the farm manager for Grainger Farms in Immokalee, said that in his 25 years in the fields he has not witnessed any cases of slavery or forced work.

Reyna said the roughly 100 workers on his farm "choose to work with our company . . . because we pay them a fair wage, offer very inexpensive housing and treat them with dignity and respect."

But Eric Schlosser, an investigative reporter and author of "Fast Food Nation," said he found it "incredible" that slavery exists in 2008, but, "I find it even more incredible that the tomato growers of Florida and some of their largest customers continue to deny that such abuses exist."

Schlosser said he believes "there are farmers that are honest and decent, but it's unfair to them to compete with those who are imposing slavery."

Committee members and panelists challenged Brown's assertion that workers could earn more than $14 an hour filling buckets that carry 32 pounds of tomatoes.

Sen. Dick Durbin, D-Ill., said workers would have to pick almost 3,000 tomatoes to earn $14 and would have to fill and empty their buckets every two minutes.

Brown acknowledged that tomato pickers may only work 20 hours a week, but Benitez said they may spend numerous unpaid hours in the field waiting for conditions to be right, and may have to return to their housing unpaid on days when it rains.

Benitez said that if Brown was serious about workers being paid $14 an hour, the pickers would accept that payment rate instead of the piecemeal rate they are currently paid.

Mary Bauer, director of the Immigrant Justice Project at the Southern Poverty Law Center, said there is "rampant abuse" of state and federal wage and hour laws in the payment of farm workers and little enforcement. She said payment rates are routinely adjusted to reflect how much crop was picked, not how much time workers were at the job.

Bauer called Brown's assertion of a $14 an hour pay rate "disingenuous . . . those statements simply aren't true in the real world."

Committee members pressed Brown on the exchange's refusal to implement agreements reached between the tomato workers and fast-food giants McDonalds and Yum! Brands— the parent company for Taco Bell, KFC, Pizza Hut and Long John Silver's—to pay workers a penny a pound extra.

Brown said the exchange did not oppose the restaurant chains paying the workers directly, but did not want to act as the middle man in determining which workers were entitled to higher payments. He said it was impossible to determine which tomato picked by which worker ultimately went to which restaurant.

Sen. Bernie Sanders, I-Vt., who chaired the hearing, said the committee planned to continue monitoring the issue.

For Further Discussion

1. What do you think motivated Huck Finn to head for the territory? Was he running from the reality of a racist society or toward a new kind of freedom? (Consult Covici, Dempsey, and Sloane.)

2. Readers of Twain's novel sharply disagree on a number of issues, especially the evasion, or last section, when Huck follows Tom's orders and Jim becomes something of a minstrel figure. How do you react to this section? Should Twain have left it out? Why or why not? (Consult Pettit, Morrison, and Smith.)

3. Another controversy surrounds Jim's reason for not telling Huck about Pap's death. Discuss all the possible reasons. (Consult Robinson.)

4. Discuss the many ways in which Jim's and Huck's situations and characters are alike. (See Fishkin and Leary.)

5. Examine all references in the book to religion, both private and organized—keeping in mind "I'll go to hell." What is Twain's verdict on a religion that justifies slavery? Is going to hell presented as a real sacrifice for Huck? (Consult Arac and Yates.)

6. In your opinion, is *Adventures of Huckleberry Finn* a racist novel or an attack on racism? (See Chadwick-Joshua, Wieck, and Smith.)

7. What is the state of racism in the United States in the first decade of the twenty-first century? (See Obama, Knaus, Merida, and Lipman.)

For Further Reading

George Washington Cable, *The Silent South*. New York: Charles Scribner's Sons, 1899.

Frederick Douglass, *The Narrative of the Life of Frederick Douglass, an American Slave*. Boston: Anti-Slavery Office, 1845.

Frances Anne Kemble, *Journal of a Residence on a Georgian Plantation in 1838–1839*. New York: Harper and Bros., 1863.

Herman Melville, "Benito Cereno," in *The Piazza Tales*. New York: Dix, Edwards, 1856.

Harriet Beecher Stowe, *Uncle Tom's Cabin; or, Life Among the Lowly*. Boston: J.P. Jewett, 1853.

Mark Twain, *The Adventures of Tom Sawyer*. Hartford, CT: American Publishing, 1876.

———, *A Connecticut Yankee in King Arthur's Court*. New York: Webster, 1889.

———, *Life on the Mississippi*. Boston: Osgood, 1883.

———, *Mark Twain's Autobiography*. Ed. Charles Neider. New York: Harper, 1959.

———, *The Prince and the Pauper*. New York: Harper, 1881.

———, *Roughing It*. Hartford, CT: American Publishing, 1872.

———, *The Tragedy of Pudd'nhead Wilson*. Hartford, CT: American Publishing, 1894.

Bibliography

Books

Gladys Carmen
Bellamy

Mark Twain as a Literary Artist.
Norman: University of Oklahoma
Press, 1950.

Walter Blair

Mark Twain and Huck Finn. Berkeley:
University of California Press, 1960.

John W.
Blassingame

*The Slave Community: Plantation Life
in the Antebellum South.* New York:
Oxford University Press, 1979.

Van Wyck Brooks

The Ordeal of Mark Twain. New
York: Dutton, 1933.

Guy Cardwell

*The Man Who Was Mark Twain:
Images and Ideologies.* New Haven,
CT: Yale University Press, 1991.

Bernard DeVoto

Mark Twain at Work. Cambridge,
MA: Harvard University Press, 1942.

T.S. Eliot

Introduction to *Adventures of
Huckleberry Finn.* Ed. Sculley Bradley
et al. New York: Norton, 1977.

Shelley Fisher
Fishkin

*Lighting Out for the Territory:
Reflections on Mark Twain and
American Culture.* New York: Oxford
University Press, 1996.

Philip S. Foner

Mark Twain: Social Critic. New York:
International Publishers, 1958.

| George Fredrickson | *The Black Image in the White Mind: The Debate on Afro-American Character and Destiny, 1817–1914.* New York: Harper and Row, 1971. |

| John C. Gerber | *Mark Twain.* Boston: Twayne Publishers, 1988. |

| John Q. Hays | *Mark Twain and Religion: A Mirror of American Eclecticism.* New York: Peter Lang, 1989. |

| Justin Kaplan | *Mr. Clemens and Mark Twain: A Biography.* New York: Simon and Schuster, 1966. |

| James S. Leonard, Thomas A. Tenney, and Thadious M. Davis, eds. | *Satire or Evasion? Black Perspectives on "Huckleberry Finn."* Durham, NC: Duke University Press, 1992. |

| Eric Lott | "Mr. Clemens and Jim Crow: Twain, Race, and Blackface," in *The Cambridge Companion to Mark Twain.* Ed. Forrest G. Robinson. New York: Cambridge University Press, 1995. |

| People for the American Way | *Attacks on the Freedom to Learn, 1993–1994.* Washington, DC: People for the American Way, 1994. |

| Lee Sigelman and Susan Welch | *Black Americans' Views of Racial Inequality: The Dream Deferred.* New York: Cambridge University Press, 1991. |

| Kenneth M. Stampp | *The Peculiar Institution: Slavery in the Ante-Bellum South.* New York: Vintage Books, 1989. |

Periodicals

William Andrews	"Mark Twain and James W.C. Pennington: Huckleberry Finn's Smallpox Lie," *Studies in American Fiction*, vol. 9, Spring 1981.
Scotty Ballard	"How to Handle Racism," *Jet*, July 29, 2002.
Walter Blair	"Why Huck and Jim Went Downstream," *College English*, vol. 18, no. 2, November 1956.
Louis Budd	"The Recomposition of *Adventures of Huckleberry Finn*," *Missouri Review*, vol. 10, no. 1, Winter 1987.
Allen Carey-Webb	"Racism and *Huckleberry Finn*: Censorship, Dialogue, and Change," *English Journal*, vol. 82, no. 7, November 1993.
Beverley P. Cole	"NAACP on *Huck Finn*: Train Teachers to Be Sensitive; Don't Censor," *Crisis*, vol. 82, October 1982.
Hugh J. Dawson	"The Ethnicity of Huck Finn—and the Difference It Makes," *American Literary Realism, 1870–1910*, vol. 30, no. 2, Winter 1998.

W.E.B. Du Bois "The Humor of Negroes," *Mark Twain Quarterly*, vol. 5, Fall/Winter 1942–1943.

Ralph Ellison "Change the Joke and Slip the Yoke," *Partisan Review*, vol. 25, Spring 1958.

Chadwick Hansen "The Character of Jim and the Ending of *Huckleberry Finn*," *Massachusetts Review*, vol. 5, Autumn 1963.

Dexter Hill "Local Newspapers Cover Rising Number of Racist Anti-Obama Actions in Small Towns," *Editor and Publisher*, November 14, 2008. www.editorandpublisher.com.

Lucinda H. MacKethan "Huck Finn and the Slave Narratives: Lighting Out as Design," *Southern Review*, vol. 20, April 1984.

New York Times "Huck Finn's Friend Jim," September 13, 1957.

Kevin Sack "In Little Rock, Clinton Warns of Racial Split," *New York Times*, September 26, 1997.

Pierre Tristam "Harvest of Shame: Florida's Modern-Day Slavery," *Daytona Beach (FL) News-Journal*, July 6, 2008.

Milton J. Valencia "Black Church in Springfield Burns. Fire Began Hours After Vote, Prompting Fears It Was Arson," *Boston Globe*, November 6, 2008.

Index